F·L·O·W·E·R·S

F·L·O·W·E·R·S

MALCOLM HILLIER

Photography by Stephen Hayward

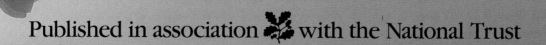

Published in association with the National Trust

DK

Dorling Kindersley

LONDON

For Colin Hilton

Art Editor Sally Smallwood
Project Editor Jane Laing
Editor Heather Dewhurst

Editorial Director Jackie Douglas
Art Director Roger Bristow

First published in Great Britain in 1988 by Dorling Kindersley
Limited, London
First paperback edition 1991

British Library Cataloguing in Publication Data
Hillier, Malcolm
Flowers.
1. Flower arrangement. Manuals
I. Title
745.92

ISBN 0-86318-745-2

Typeset in Perpetua by MFK Typesetting Ltd, Hitchin,
Hertfordshire
Colour reproduction by Colourscan Co. Pte Ltd, Singapore
Printed and bound in Hong Kong by Wing King Tong Co. Ltd

Contents

Graham Thomas, formerly the National Trust's Gardens' Adviser, recently wrote: "One of the ideas of having flowers or foliage in rooms is to decorate them for an 'occasion'. Alternatively, some dedicated flower lovers will have vases holding a few special blooms simply to admire them at close quarters. In either case they add grace, colour and charm to a room when gently arranged." It is Malcolm Hillier's flair for creating arrangements which are gentle and natural that makes them eminently suitable for the houses of many differing periods and sizes that belong to the National Trust.

The Trust's rooms are always open for an "occasion" and its policy is to follow, where possible, the traditions of each house, with flowers and plants raised in the gardens and arranged by the house or garden staff.

At Petworth, for instance, large bowls of mixed cut flowers are arranged in the style and taste set in the 1960s by Lady Egremont. At Chartwell, flowers favoured by Lady Churchill continue to be grown in the garden and glasshouses and disposed around the house as she preferred.

Flower cultivation in medieval times was chiefly confined to the gardens of monasteries and large demesnes, where they were grown with the vegetables primarily for medicines and cosmetics but also for making decorative garlands. At Cotehele, the Great Hall is still decorated throughout December with a garland nearly 30m (100ft) long made of yew, holly and ivy interwoven with statice, honesty and other dried flowers.

From nosegays to tulips

In Tudor times the pleasure garden appeared with its knots, beds and quarters filled with flowers. In one quarter would be grown "herbs and flowers used to make nosegaies . . . whose colours being glorious and different are wondrous to behold", and in another quarter "all sweet smelling herbs". Clippings from the herbs and knot edgings were added to the rushes strewn over floors, and the version of Holbein's "Sir Thomas More and his family", which hangs at Nostell Priory, shows how flowers were used to decorate a room. Three vases containing irises, lilies, paeonies, carnations and columbines are on the windowsill and buffet, and at this time the chimney piece might have been filled with "a fine bank of moss or aspen and at either end Rosemary Pots".

Nosegays, or "tussie mussies", were carried to ward off bad smells and pestilence. This custom continued until the Victorian era when no woman was considered properly dressed in company without one, and their aid to courtship was considerable when each flower could convey a message, a jonquil crying out "have pity on my passion". In the grander houses during the 1600s the flowers were often banished from the main garden with its grand walls, grass plots and parterres, but the smaller flower garden still tumbled with roses, hollyhocks, sweet williams, auriculas and, from 1629, the fragrant tuberoses introduced from Mexico. At a banquet at Knole in July 1636, the servants were ordered by Lord Sackville to put "sweet briar, stock, gilly flowers, pinks, wall flowers and any other sweet flowers in glasses and pots (vases) in every window and chimney".

In the 1650s, Sir Ralph Verney, imprisoned in St James's Palace for his royalist sympathies, undeterred was arranging for tulips, pinks and gilly flowers to be sent to Claydon from Holland and France. From these countries came the fashion for arranging them in a tall, upright manner. Usually a crown imperial, lily, iris or sunflower would be a centrepiece at the top with a mixture of large and small flowers jostling for position below it. An exquisite woodcarving by Grinling Gibbons at Petworth shows such an arrangement.

The tulip, passionately admired in England since the 1630s, came truly into its own with the accession of Dutch William and his Stuart queen in 1688. Handsome blue and white pyramid vases of delftware, some 160cm (5ft) high, were used to display the blooms, and the Trust has examples of these at Dyrham and Lytes Cary.

The unarranged look

From about 1720 "glorious irregularity" was blurring the strict boundaries of the formal garden. This extended to the house, too, where flowers sometimes looked as though they had been hurriedly crammed into vases. Batty Langley in *New Principles of Gardening* suggested flowers in the house should be arranged in a "free loose manner, so as not to represent a stiff bundle of flowers void of freedom, in which the beauty of everything consists".

By the middle of the century most of the gentry had a rural retreat where country pursuits could be enjoyed. While the gentlemen managed and improved their farms, the ladies occupied themselves with their gardens. In August 1748, Mrs Delany wrote that she was in the garden

every morning by 7 o'clock and most of the day besides. "My flower garden is a wilderness of flowers, the beds are overpowered with them," she declared.

Filling the house with flowers

With improved roads and better sprung carriages came an increase in visiting and entertaining, which contributed to a greater interest in "decking out" the house with flowers. The porcelain manufacturers provided a whole variety of vases to contain them. At Waddesdon, the collection of Sèvres includes vases, bulb pots, jardinières and orange tubs, some in pairs and sets of three for chimney pieces, and all could be used for growing or cut flowers.

Exquisite porcelain and silver flowers with gilt stems were made for the seasons when real flowers were scarce. At Fenton House there are miniature porcelain pots and tubs complete with flowers.

Often, vases of flowers would be placed in front of a looking glass, or at night by an unshuttered window for the same effect. At Petworth, where interiors painted by Zoffany have inspired the redecoration of the bedrooms, flowers are always placed on the dressing tables, as was usual at that time. Furnishing the chimney piece was of particular importance in the eighteenth century. At Wimpole, a painting of a dog by John Wootton (c.1715) shows a vase of mixed cut flowers in the fireplace, and they would even be put inside the hob grate.

At Osterley, the state rooms have been arranged to represent their appearance at the end of the eighteenth century. Geraniums and marigolds are sometimes placed in pots decorated in black and white chalk with neo-classical ornament, and are set on stands in the gallery and on staging in the dressing room made by Robert Adam.

Changing fashions in gardens and flowers

By the last quarter of the century, landscapes had taken precedence over flower beds, which were banished some distance from the house and hidden behind walls and trees. But at the beginning of the nineteenth century, Humphry Repton brought them back close to the house. He designed gardens not only for great country houses but for more modest villas now springing up around cities.

There was no shortage of advice for these new owners from authors like John Loudon, his wife Jane and many others on how flowers and plants should be arranged and placed around the house.

Until this time, furniture had been set round the edges of a room, but from about 1810 sofas were swung out from the walls, sofa tables were set beside them, and a round table made its appearance in the middle of the room. These tables and numerous flower stands provided new positions for flowers to be viewed and enjoyed from all angles.

At the beginning of Victoria's reign, the bright hues of geraniums, begonias, and lobelias were all the rage. At Waddesdon they were "bedded out" in their thousands and described by a friend of the Rothschild family as "all perfectly dazzling".

Indoors, dahlias, fuchsias, hydrangeas and water lilies filled the glass bowls and tall flared vases of the period. Entire greenhouses were devoted to orchids or to palm trees. Palms and ferns were the hallmark of the Victorian drawing room and at Stourhead even large rhododendrons were brought into the house, later to be planted out in the garden, where they flower to this day. No wonder William Morris commented, "I have seen many a drawing room where it appeared to me less a room than a thicket".

But from the 1850s, the old-fashioned flowers were back in fashion. At Wallington, Pauline Trevelyan and her pre-Raphaelite friends were decorating the central hall with paintings of foxgloves, columbines, poppies, irises, lilies, hollyhocks and sunflowers. These were the flowers that now filled the vases of many Victorian ladies and were lovingly transplanted from cottage gardens.

Decorating with flowers

A glimpse of the Edwardian scene is given by the gardener to Mrs Greville at Polesden Lacey. She gave him orders from her bed. Lilies-of-the-valley and violets were her favourite flowers and she insisted that the latter be made to flower in November. Flowers for cutting had to be grown under glass in the winter months and included 1,000 carnations, 200 begonias and 200 poinsettias.

At Cliveden between the wars, one of the greenhouse gardeners was employed as "decorator". He has described how he had to arrange the flowers in the house three times a day, and travel to London with flowers for the house in St James's Square. He received his orders directly from Lady Astor. "Mixed flowers were her speciality, she would have them mixed. For Ascot week you wanted an enormous amount of stuff. For Christmas it had to be poinsettias six feet tall . . . the festooning took a fortnight to prepare; it was the butler's worry if it got crisp and dry (if there was a fire it would go like tinder). The big hall was festooned from corner to corner . . . it was a terrific job."

Capturing the past

Recently there has been a revival of interest in music played on early instruments and recipes culled from old cookery books. Flower arranging offers another interest, and an appreciation of how plants were used for decoration and enjoyment in the past can be drawn from the records, gardens, pictures and furnishings of homes in the care of the National Trust. (See p.256 for further information.)

Mary Rose Blacker

A floral calendar of many of my favourite flowers.

Spring

Apple blossom It seems wicked to cut, but a few sprigs of apple blossom both look and smell delicious, especially when mixed with some bluebells.

Bluebells

Camellias

Catkins A tall vase containing catkins and irises makes a striking spring arrangement.

Cherry blossom

Daffodils These bright flowers epitomize spring and look beautiful in arrangements combined with pussy willow and other narcissus.

Easter lilies White lilies are traditionally used for altar arrangements at Easter.

Forsythia

Grape hyacinths

Hyacinths

Jonquils These sweetly scented early spring narcissus are beautiful by themselves.

Lenten roses

Lilac Use lilac with ranunculus and white narcissus for May Day party arrangements, or for spring wedding arrangements.

Lilies-of-the-valley These are much loved in wedding bouquets for their scent and their bell-flowered spires.

Mimosa

Narcissus Use in bouquets for Mother's Day, by themselves or mixed with tulips and irises.

Pansies

Polyanthus

Primroses Plant a basket of primroses in moss ready for the first day of spring.

Primulas There are many pot primulas available from flower shops in spring and they make a pretty thank-you present or kitchen windowsill arrangement.

Pussy willow Also known as palm as it is used as a counterpart to palm fronds in northern countries. Arrange a vase of it with some daffodils for Palm Sunday, the Sunday before Easter.

Ranunculus

Rhododendrons

Scillas

Solomon's seal The secretive fronds of these plants with their beautiful bell flowers mix well with pink-centred narcissus.

Star of Bethlehem

Tulips Parrot tulips are the most exotic kind and they look well on their own in a bouquet for a spring birthday present.

Violets

Summer

Baby's breath Encircling any other flowers in a wedding bouquet or posy, baby's breath creates a fine, romantic mist.

Bachelor's buttons

Beech

Bells of Ireland The vivid green of these plants mixes well with most summer flowers.

Broom

Buttercups These are delightful when mixed with bachelor's buttons, ox-eye daisies and lady's mantle for an early summer nosegay.

Carnations Garland the canopy in the synagogue with pink carnations, white roses and a froth of lady's mantle for an early summer wedding.

Clematis

Columbines For a mid-summer's party al fresco mix columbines with paeonies, roses and cow parsley to make a full-blown table arrangement.

Copper beech

Cornflowers

Cow parsley Once given the hot-water treatment (see p.42) cow parsley looks superb in garlanding and pew-end arrangements for a wedding.

Daisies

Delphiniums For a very special present mix delphiniums with foxgloves and fennel.

Fennel

Foxgloves

Gerberas

Godetias A bunch of these silk-like flowers will last a long time.

Hollyhocks Mid to late summer is the best time to use these flowers, which evoke the atmosphere of a seventeenth-century flower painting.

Hostas

Iceland poppies

Irises

Laburnum

Lady's mantle

Lavender

Lilies The scented lily trumpets will light up a large fireplace arrangement in high summer. Mix them with delphiniums and larkspur and bright green summer foliage.

Love-in-a-mist For a summery present for a loved one, give a basket of roses mixed with love-in-a-mist and lavender.

Lupins

Magnolias The waxy flowers of *Magnolia grandiflora* open in mid to late summer. A bud picked in the evening will open the following day, scenting the whole house in a morning.

Marguerites

Mock orange

Monkshood

Nasturtiums Decorate summer salads with delicious-tasting nasturtium flowers in their many bright colours.

Spring

Winter

Summer

Oak

Decorative onions

Oriental poppies Heat-seal the stems of poppies (see p.41) before arranging them with red roses and red clove carnations for a ruby wedding gift.

Paeonies

Pinks

Poppies

Roses

Rosemary

Rue

Spurge

Statice

Sweet peas The early summer stems of sweet peas are the longest, and make a special thank-you present.

Sweet williams

Tobacco plant For a summer dinner party held outside make sweet-scented arrangements with tobacco flowers, pinks and clove-scented carnations.

Whitebeam For a silver wedding anniversary in early summer, make arrangements with whitebeam, white roses, mock orange and white delphiniums.

Yarrow

──────Autumn──────

Anemones Although available all year round from flower shops, the early autumn anemones are particularly good.

Artichokes

Asters

Bear's breeches

Bulrushes These form a striking arrangement with Chinese lanterns and bear's breeches for a party or reception.

China asters

Chinese lanterns

Chrysanthemums These flowers epitomize autumn. Use them by themselves or mixed with belladonna lilies and hydrangeas

for special occasions.

Dahlias As the weather makes the garden less attractive, bring in the dahlias and arrange them by themselves in jugs.

Dock

Fuchsias

Gladioli These flowers look best arranged on their own in a tall vase for an autumn lunch party.

Golden rod For harvest festival, decorate the church with golden and rust arrangements, using golden rod, dahlias, gladioli and chrysanthemums.

Gourds

Hydrangeas Use a head of hydrangea flowers as a basis for an autumn wedding posy, threading through other small flowers like kaffir lilies and nerines and tying the stems with ribbons or lengths of raffia.

Ice plant

Kaffir lilies

Love-lies-bleeding

Michaelmas daisies Give a Michaelmas Day's dinner party and decorate the house with jugs of Michaelmas daisies.

Montbretia

Nerines These delicate flowers look well in autumn wedding bouquets when mixed with cream freesias and roses, ivy trails and rosemary.

Red hot pokers

Rowan berries

St John's wort

Scabious

Vine

Wheat Make up a harvest table for harvest thanksgiving with a wheat sheaf, baskets of apples and autumn fruits, and golden flower and berry arrangements.

Zinnias

──────Winter──────

Amaryllis Use amaryllis to make stunning arrangements

with other lilies for a Jewish New Year present.

Aucuba

Box

Christmas roses Bring a few of these in from the garden to make an informal arrangement for the Christmas holiday.

Cones

Dogwood

Elaeagnus The variegation of *Elaeagnus pungens* 'Maculata' makes it a favourite to be used with Christmas evergreen garlanding and holly, blue spruce and larch cone twigs.

Fatsia

Heather It is lovely to use some flowering white heather for luck in a winter wedding bouquet. Mix it with yellow spray carnations and Christmas roses.

Holly A berried sprig makes the ideal festive topping for the Christmas pudding.

Ivy

Juniper Arrange bowls of juniper and berried ivy with colourful flowers from the florist for a New Year's Eve party.

Laurel

Mahonia

Poinsettias These plants have now become traditional gifts at Christmas time. Try arranging smaller plants with cut flowers for stunning effect.

Red roses Hot-house grown red roses are the favoured flower to give on Valentine's Day, as they mean "I love you".

Snowdrops A little bunch of snowdrops make a beautiful present for a child to give.

Wintersweet

Witch hazel On a mild winter's day pick witch hazel, daphne and wintersweet from the garden and bring them in to perfume the living room.

Autumn

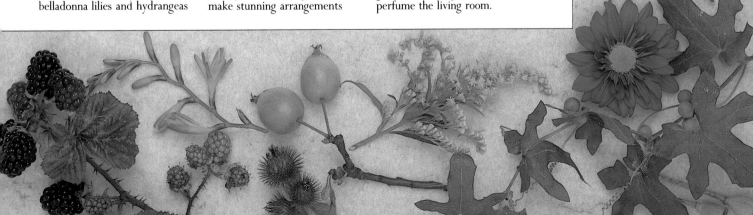

Introduction

Since the beginning of time flowers have been used to celebrate. They are appropriate to so many different occasions, so many different feelings and experiences. A simple bunch given to a friend or someone you love is magical. A decoration in the home for a special occasion adds a special touch. In times of happiness flowers can blaze with pomp and glory, jostle noisily with fun; in serenity, they can be tranquil, and in times of sadness they can be a solace. Flowers are a comfort and an expression of joy, with a beauty that brightens the most ordinary or miserable of days.

The ancient Chinese attributed special meanings to the various plants that grew wild in the countryside and to those that they cultivated. They used flowers in religious rituals. Originally each of their flower arrangements contained only one type of flower. In spring the paeony and peach blossom were most popular; the lotus epitomized summer, and the chrysanthemum, autumn. Plum blossom, paper white narcissus and pine branches were frequently used in winter. The early Egyptians designed special vases for their flowers and often decorated the vases with flower motifs. The Greeks and the Romans always incorporated flowers into their celebrations. They used leaves and flowers in their religious ceremonies, making headdresses, wreaths and garlands for brides and grooms, and for heroes and athletes victorious from the wars or games. Sometimes, for an assembly, they would strew a whole floor with scented rose petals.

Floral customs

Flowers have played a part in many festive seasons around the world, and many floral customs continue to this day. In most of the countries of the far east, flower-heads are strung together to make necklaces, often sweetly scented, which are worn on special occasions by both men and women. In Hawaii and Fiji these necklaces are traditionally given to visitors, and tourists are now garlanded as a symbol of welcome as they step from their 'plane.

In northern climes, May Day has been celebrated with flowers since pagan times, when the maypole dance originated. A tall pole is garlanded with flowers and a group of dancers with flower circlets in their hair encircle it, each holding a ribbon that loops up to the top of the pole. They gradually twist their ribbons as they dance, to make interlaced patterns down the length of the pole. In mid-winter, boughs of greenery and berries were traditionally brought into the house, and holly, ivy and mistletoe continue to be used for decorations at Christmas time, which falls near the time of the old pagan ceremony.

The raising of the garlanded maypole was a common scene in the countryside on May Day, the first of May (left), as was the dancing that followed.
An arrangement in seventeenth-century Flemish style, using flowers from different seasons (right).

—PLANT MATERIAL—
Lilies, amaryllis, irises, eucomis, hollyhocks, hydrangea, vine, delphiniums, carnations, tulips, tobacco plant, everlasting peas, chicory, roses, nerines, poppies, peaches and pomegranate

All over the world flowers are an important part of wedding ceremonies. At Jewish weddings, the bride and groom are married under a canopy, which is frequently garlanded and festooned with flowers. Arrangements of flowers are usually part of the festivities after the ceremony. The decoration of the synagogue or church with arrangements of flowers is a great statement of joy and happiness, which is so appropriate to this very special occasion.

A growing art

In the west, the art of arranging flowers was first documented in the seventeenth century, when the Dutch, in particular, painted wonderful informal arrangements. I find these a tremendous inspiration, especially in their use not only of the flowers and foliage, but of fruit and vegetables as well. These are the arrangements that I enjoy creating best. I love to choose a great mixture of brilliantly colourful and scented flowers and combine them with beautiful-looking fruits, such as pineapples, pomegranates, mulberries and crab apples and maybe some common or garden vegetables with interesting shapes, like curly kale, cabbage, beans or peppers.

In the eighteenth century, many potteries produced vases for flowers as well as china for the table. Wedgwood and Sèvres are the most famous among many other makers of ceramics during this period. Arrangements were used to decorate the houses of wealthier families and the aristocracy on a regular basis. Vases of flowers sat on the newly introduced mantelshelves, and in summer a vase of flowers was placed in the fireplace, standing on the hearth. Arrangements were also placed on tables, which had now been brought into the body of the room.

A two-tier epergne with delicate spring flowers.

In Britain, the most popular flowers in summer were roses, carnations, irises, paeonies, delphiniums, monkshood and hollyhocks. Although the chrysanthemum was introduced from China to the west at this time, it was not until a century later that it became a popular flower, and was used to decorate the house in all manner of flower arrangements.

Plants introduced and developed

The Victorians loved their plants and flowers, and it was during the nineteenth century that the majority of plant introductions took place. The Victorians were great collectors and also great hybridizers. They brought to England and America many plants from China, Africa and South America. Some of them – like rhododendrons, azaleas, tree paeonies, roses, gladioli and chrysanthemums – have become favourite garden plants. Others – like begonias, calceolarias and fuchsias – were grown in conservatories and bedded out for the summer months.

Plants like carnations and auriculas were developed in their thousands to produce very fancy striped and blotched varieties. Roses were crossed to produce fabulous great blooms with a great number of petals, and most of them

A wild arrangement.

were wonderfully scented as well. Nosegays were extremely fashionable at the beginning of Victoria's long reign. A pretty bunch of flowers was always carried to a special social event. It was at this time, too, that the meaning of the flowers in a posy or nosegay took on such importance. Every imaginable plant and flower was given a meaning. Some of these related directly to the look of the flowers; for instance, a thistle meant retaliation, a dahlia, pomp, and a mock orange represented counterfeit. Some of the meanings were attributed by looking back to flowers mentioned earlier in biblical times; a white lily stood for purity because it was associated in the bible with the Virgin Mary. Yet others seem to have been pure inventions, conjured up to give special meaning where there was none. Whichever the case, I am sure that everyone had a lot of fun communicating intentions and emotions with a few simple flowers. Flowers became a code for a time when feelings could not be expressed directly.

Informal and elaborate arrangements

The Victorians retained an informality of style in their flower arrangements, resulting in some very beautiful and romantic arrangements, in the manner of those painted by Fantin Latour. You seem to be able to smell the perfume of the old roses in rustic baskets that he painted. Not only did Victorian ladies use tremendous mixtures of flowers in their arrangements, but frequently they placed only one type of flower in a vase, either by itself or combined with a few stems of interesting foliage such as ferns, ornamental grasses and even bulrushes. It was at this time that different colours were combined for the first time, often very successfully, and many of these colour schemes are still used today. The combination of white, scarlet and maroon, together with

A lustrous jug makes a perfect vessel for this group of mixed old-fashioned roses that seem naturally to grow upwards and outwards.

—**PLANT MATERIAL**—
**Pale pink, deep pink, cream
and yellow old-fashioned
roses**

*A*lmost any mix of flowers would look attractive in this silver-paper-lined vase, but the silver foliage provides a strong unifying link. The few bright green leaves and the orange montbretia enliven and add magic to the whole arrangement.

**PLANT
—MATERIAL—**
Artemisia, Japanese anemones, delphiniums, everlasting sweet peas, spindle, blackberries, pearl everlasting, phlox, roses, montbretia, yarrow, euphorbia, veronica and globe amaranth

shades of green foliage, was one peculiar to this time.

In the second half of the nineteenth century, many books were published on the subject of flower arranging. They contained illustrations of elaborate and wild decorations for dinner parties and special seasonal occasions, including wonderful garlands and swags, and many tiered epergnes for sideboards or dinner tables. Even Mrs Beeton's *Household Management* includes mention of flower arrangements: "We can imagine no household duty more attractive to the ladies of the house than that of making their tables beautiful with the exquisite floral produce of the different seasons, exercising their taste in devising new ways of employing the materials at their command. Young people should have their taste for arranging flowers encouraged, and be allowed to assist in decorating the table. Care should be taken not to overload the table with flowers."

At this time, enthusiasm and interest in flower arranging was also developing apace in America, where new, brighter colours and shapes of flowers were becoming available, such as dahlias and nasturtiums, azaleas and camellias. At a time when there were few leisure occupations open for women outside the home, women's magazines contained plenty of advice on looking after and displaying cut flowers. It soon became the norm to have flower arrangements placed in every room.

Learning from the Impressionists

Around the turn of the century magical flower arrangements became subjects of the paintings of the Impressionists, from Van Gogh with his famous "Sunflowers" to Cezanne, and from Bonnard, with a bombardment of rich colour, and the more restrained flowers painted by Vuillard and Degas to Manet and Monet, with the wonderful paintings of flowers, Monet's garden and water lilies. Their arrangements portray flowers in a completely different and incredibly beautiful way. They suggest the scent, the colour and mood of the arrangements rather than painting a realistic representation as previous generations of painters had done.

Absolute favourites of mine and a great influence on me are the flower paintings of Odilon Redon, which were mostly painted in the early part of this century. In these paintings, the container and flowers are very closely associated and the colours seem to spring from

A silver wine cooler makes a gleaming container for this great mix of sunny coloured flowers. The informal, wild look of the arrangement is accentuated by the crooked stems and hanging flowers.

**PLANT
—MATERIAL—**
Iceland poppies, roses, amaryllis, parrot tulips, Guelder roses, carnations, snapdragons, broom, cow parsley, arum lilies and smilax

the canvas in thrilling mixtures of bright reds and oranges, intense blues and pinks, with touches of lemon-yellow and white.

Although some of the flowers that Redon painted are imaginary – and many rather fantastic – it is easy to relate them to roses, cow parsley, paeonies, delphiniums, Chinese lanterns, honesty and anemones, and it is not impossible to create arrangements with a very similar feel and mood. The vases he painted seem just as much part of the arrangement as the flowers, and their colours are frequently very strongly related.

The plentitude of summer

Early summer is the very best time of year for flowers. Suddenly, in gardens and flower shops, too, there is a wonderful array of flowers: roses, paeonies, delphiniums and sweet peas fill the air with their scents and colours. Three exciting months of summer flowers follow.

Colours are both at their richest and most subtle in summer: reds and blues, peaches and apricots and creams, deep and pale yellows are all offset by the brilliant greens of glistening fresh foliage. Summer is also the time of silver and lilac and pink: the heat-hazy colours of distant hills. It is the time of the sun-baked aromatic scents of rosemary, lavender, santolina and eucalyptus and that most delicious and surprising scent of all – iris. Summer is the time to use unashamedly all the colours of the spectrum, except perhaps orange, which should be used sparingly.

The colours of autumn and winter

As strawberries belong to summer, so orange and rust belong to autumn. The colours of bonfires and the setting sun are the colours of autumn flowers. In early and mid-winter, flowers are very scarce. Gardens take on a gaunt greyness that is almost unrelieved, but not quite. Popping up in the gloom are a few sprigs of winter jasmine, the pale, crisp white moon glow of Christmas rose, and in the milder districts, the blossom of winter cherry, *Prunus subhirtella autumnalis*, the scented flower-heads of some of the viburnums, and the yellow spires of *Mahonia japonica*.

All of a sudden the greyness begins to lift and soon after yellows and white abound. To echo the spring skies there are touches of clear blue in hyacinths, with their magical scent, scillas and early irises.

I especially love the flowers of early summer, and of these I would choose the paeonies, sweet peas and the old roses. They seem to epitomize the promise of summer, with their opulent massed petals and their deliciously sweet fragrances. They make glorious presents arranged in the simplest bunch. They also look lovely in a posy, where the flowers are arranged to be seen from all round as well as in a more formal bouquet, which has a flatter back.

—PLANT MATERIAL—
Roses, lilies, mock orange, paeonies, allium, asparagus, clematis, escallonia, hosta leaves, love-in-a-mist and irises

*I*t is always possible to make up lovely arrangements from flowers of different seasons. For instance, my favourite flowers, lilies, as well as chrysanthemums, are available all year round from flower shops. This sunny arrangement in blue, white and yellow — colours that always look deliciously fresh together — is also full of fragrance, with its great white auratum lilies and white fronds of lilac, though the yellow roses are only faintly scented.

**PLANT
—MATERIAL—
Roses, lilies,
delphiniums,
chrysanthemums,
camellia foliage and
lilac**

Flowers available out of season

The Flemish and Italian artists of the seventeenth century used artistic licence to fill their vases with myriad flowers from all the seasons, but today we can do nearly as well in reality, as more and more flowers become readily available all year round.

Flower shops carry not only seasonal flowers but many beautiful and exotic flowers from around the world, so that those long-lasting spray chrysanthemums – which are now grown in many countries – are available all year round. So are tulips from Holland, roses of all colours, and carnations and spray carnations, which come from as far afield as Columbia and Greece. Irises, freesias, gypsophila – all these and many more – are available throughout all the seasons, making it possible to create arrangements that have a particular style and colour range. Even so, it is always a good plan, and much more interesting, to keep arrangements seasonal whenever possible. This is the way to achieve the most natural-looking arrangements. Try to resort to the out-of-season, all-year-round flowers only when absolutely essential for the sort of arrangement you wish to create.

The hues and shades of flowers

If there are any rules about using colours in flower arrangements then the seasonal ones are the only rules that I know: a great bright mix of colours in summer, warm, mellow hues in autumn, harder lines of browns with dark greens for winter and clear white, yellows and blues in spring.

Like any rules, they can often be broken to good effect. In fact, it is simple to play safe with colour and combine flowers of colours that are close to each other in the spectrum. You cannot go far wrong by mixing red and orange, or orange and yellow, yellow and green, green and blue or blue and violet. But the further apart in the spectrum of colours are your flowers, the more daring you must be.

At the reverse end of the scale, mixtures of yellow and violet, and orange and blue can look stunning. These combinations are much more daring, and should be exploited occasionally.

There are few colours that look awful together. Maybe some differing blues look uncomfortable when juxtaposed, and dull orange can be difficult to use successfully as it often seems to remove the clarity of other colours near to it.

Green is the odd man out in the colour spectrum as far as plant material is concerned because it is the colour of foliage. It always seems to exist happily with any of the other colours. In fact, it strengthens and vitalizes other colours, particularly those that are strong in tone, such as red, bright blue and yellow.

The importance of foliage
The greens of foliage are tremendously important in arrangements. They bring to life the colours of the flowers with which they are arranged. There are so many different shades to choose from: the golden yellow greens of elaeagnus, euonymus, privet and griselinia; the rich, bright greens of beech, oak, fern fronds, palm leaves, pittosporum, camellia and rhododendron; the silvery green leaves of rosemary, *Senecio* 'Sunshine', lavender, santolina and artemisia; and the dark heavy greens of yew, box and holly.

Leaf shapes vary enormously, from the fine needles of pine to the complicated lattice-work fronds of fern, and from the large-fingered leaves of fig to the feathery leaves of mountain ash. All add their special mark to an arrangement. Indeed, an arrangement featuring only foliage can look splendid.

*F*oliage is often even more varied in shape and form than the flowers. This foliage arrangement takes both form and colour from its vase: there are combinations of stripes, curves, spikes and clusters in a wide range of colours.

—PLANT MATERIAL—
Bells of Ireland, fan palm, angel wings, gaultheria, oats and milkweed

I like to use a lot of green, especially the foliage of the flowers in the arrangement. It is better to limit the flowers than the foliage, as foliage gives a natural growing look to every arrangement. It offsets the forms and colours of the flowers that it is mixed with just as it does in the countryside or garden, where green is always the predominant colour, even during the winter months.

Flowers and their containers

Every flower arrangement that we create in a container is like a three-dimensional painting set on the wall of a room, and it is the *whole* effect of the flowers and container, and their relationship to the surroundings that is important. Flower arrangements have an advantage over still-life paintings, though: they do not last for ever. In fact, they last for probably only a week, so there is no chance of becoming bored with them.

The combination of flowers and container is crucial to the success of the arrangement. Sometimes flowers will cry out for a particular container and sometimes a container will immediately suggest a selection of flowers to be arranged in it. So the coffee cup decorated with roses on page 150 seems perfect filled with

A flower garden in an ornate dish.

matching old-fashioned roses. Equally, the lavender and clary look especially attractive in a basket made from lavender stems (see p.226). Maybe it will be the colours and texture of a container that suggest which flowers to use in the arrangement, such as the flowers used in the Janice Tchalenko jug on page 153. Of course, it is not always possible to fill a container with exactly the flowers it demands, but it is good to try.

I love arrangements where the container and the flowers seem absolutely meant for each other; where

—PLANT MATERIAL—
Red hot pokers, snapdragons, yarrow, dahlia and ivy

It is not always the most obvious container that makes for the most interesting arrangement. Here the spout of a watering can echoes the shapes of the flowers.

colours and forms complement each other, from the shape and decorations of the vase to the flowers and leaves themselves. Certainly, there are many containers that are unexacting.

Many combinations of flowers will look good in ceramic vases in shades of white. However, shape is important here. Allow the form of the vase to dictate the shape of the arrangement. A bulbous goldfish bowl of a vase invariably requires a generously curved creation, whereas a tall, straight-sided vase demands tall, straight spires of flowers. This is not to say that it would be impossible to do the reverse, but it is safer to follow this guide.

Gathering vases and baskets

I like to keep a collection of vases to which I am always adding new ones. I keep a constant look-out for simple household receptacles, such as cups, mugs, jugs, wastepaper baskets and casseroles, and I have some inexpensive cracked pieces of china from the eighteenth and nineteenth centuries. They can always be lined if they leak and I do not mind the cracks if the vase is beautiful.

Baskets always look attractive filled with flowers, especially the more rustic, twiggy ones, which are made all over the world. All sorts of plant material are used to make these baskets, from the traditional willow to scented thyme and lavender branches, and from olive and bamboo to palm and vines. A basket *is* plant material, and that is why other plant material looks so appropriate in a basket.

The range of ceramics you can use is enormous. In general, I find that plain-coloured vases or those with

These flowers seem to be growing naturally out of stone.

abstract or geometric designs, rather than those that are over-decorated with flowers, are the most satisfactory in which to create arrangements. If you have an attractively shaped vase with an ugly pattern or design, remember that you can cover it with some cloth or plant material (see p.39).

Terracotta pots also make decorative containers. Because terracotta is porous, however, it will be necessary to line the container with plastic. Wooden containers also need to be lined in this way. Their rustic quality serves as a suitable companion to simple country flowers.

Glass is a wonderful medium for flowers. I love clear glass containers in which the flower stems are visible; sometimes, depending on the shape of the vase, the stems become magnified. It is not always so easy to find metal and stone containers, though you may have a wine cooler, attractive biscuit or tea tin or stone mortar tucked away in the kitchen that can be brought into service as a flower container.

Following nature

The natural look is always the most attractive, and it is always best to avoid using a supporting medium like foam or chicken-wire where it is possible to use the sides, base or rim of a vase to do the job. Incurving vases offer plenty of support but if the vase opens outwards, or if the vase is shallow, support for the stems can be a problem.

The more an arrangement resembles growing plants the more beautiful it is. An arrangement must encapsulate a plant or a group of plants growing together. So it is always worth keeping an eye open for interesting and unusual combinations of plants that can often be found, either growing wild in the fields, hedgerows or woods, or cultivated varieties abounding in gardens everywhere.

Here are three different-shaped containers to be used for a variety of arrangements: a flat glass-handled dish, a decorative cup and a Chinese-shaped vase.

A fine china Belleek cup and saucer make the perfect container for these exciting little flowers. The green of the spurge and the white of the pea echo the shamrock on the white transparent glaze.

—PLANT MATERIAL—
Spurge, everlasting pea, lavender, wild pansy, cotton lavender, tricyrtis, dead nettle and mint

Most plants grow with a strong central form, which is then broken up in a random way by shoots with leaves or flower spikes. They frequently look like curved-topped mounds. So it is with arrangements. The basic form must have strength to it: the curves need to be good, strong curves, and the straight lines well defined. This strong form can then be broken up by foliage, branches, twigs and flowers, so that it becomes interesting, while retaining its basic shape.

The container approximates to the bed or ground that the arrangement grows from, and it must be in harmony with the flowers. In turn, the whole creation must be in harmony with its surroundings and relate to the space in which it is to stand.

If the arrangement is to stand against a wall or mirror where it is to be seen only from the front and the sides then it probably needs to have a flat back, like an open fan. If it is to be free standing, then it will need to be an all-round arrangement, so that it can be viewed from all angles. The general rule is that the overall creation should be about three times the height of the container and twice as wide. But this is only a rough guide, and many beautiful, well-proportioned arrangements do not follow this at all.

Considering the setting

Before starting to create an arrangement of flowers, think about where you want to position it and how it will relate to the designs, colours, forms and textures around it. Consider the space that will surround the arrangement and how that space is used. This will give you an idea of the scale and size the arrangement should be. If it is to stand on a hallway table, then it must be large enough to be noticed, but it must not be so wide that it obstructs the free passage of people walking through the hall.

If the arrangement is to go on a dining table, then it must look attractive from the points of view of all the diners, and it must not take up too much of the table, making the place settings or serving areas cramped. Most importantly, it must not obstruct the view of the guests sitting opposite one another. This does not necessarily mean that it cannot be tall, but if it is tall it almost certainly needs to be narrow, with the flowers held above eye-level, rather like an epergne.

If it is for a bedside table then it must not take up all the room. Leave space for a book and for leaning across in the dark to check the time or turn off the alarm.

Arrangements in the kitchen must not interfere with the workings of the cook and, although it is really nice to have flowers in the kitchen, they should be out of the way, perhaps on a shelf or windowsill.

There is always a place for flowers in any room, however large, small or difficult to situate, be it on a shelf or table, a cupboard top or pedestal or the floor.

An arrangement for a coffee table should look good from above and either side. It should not take up too much room: you may want to place coffee cups on the table after dinner. A shelf arrangement should not look cramped beneath the shelf above it. Remember that in any situation, the flowers should always have space to declare themselves attractively. An arrangement for a fireplace rarely looks good fitted into the grate of the fire. It is much better to stand it on the hearth in front of the grate. Remember that it will probably be seen from the sides as well as the front.

Matching the decorations

Always take into account the atmosphere of the room. Chrome and modern glass rarely look attractive in a Victorian or chintzy setting, whereas they can look very special against old well patinated wood, such as oak, as well as in a modern room. If the decorations are sombre, rich-coloured flowers and containers look best. In a pastel room, pale-coloured flowers, with touches of bright colour, make an ideal arrangement.

Although an arrangement should relate to the style and decoration of the room in which it is placed, I think that there is something too calculated about matching flowers to decorations exactly. The Japanese know a great deal about this. While, for the most part, their arrangements do not look right in a western setting, they understand that no arrangement should be too perfect. I like to see the odd flower that has dropped its petals as flowers growing in the garden do; the odd spot of interestingly different colour, like a cunning weed that has flowered amongst a carefully designed group of plants in a border.

A large black basket makes just the right container for this grand arrangement on the hearth in front of an empty summer grate. The bright shining white of the flowers illuminates the white walls and sparkling mirrors in the room.

—PLANT MATERIAL—
Lilies, phlox, mock orange, snapdragons, foxtail lilies, paeonies and cow parsley

Echo and offset the colours of your rooms with your flowers, simply by avoiding using colours that seem to you to look unattractive together. Different shades of blue flowers seem to do nothing but kill each other. Sky-blue becomes less sky-like if set against a lilac-blue, and is even less like the sky when set against a turquoise, although fortunately there are very few turquoise flowers in the world. Yet turquoise is a wonderful colour when mixed with creams and lemons, reds, oranges, rusts and dark greens.

Sometimes, it will be the colour of the wood in your room or the pattern of your curtains, carpet or wallpaper that gives you the idea for a combination of flowers. Other times it will be the mix of flowers outside in the garden. Whatever prompts you to arrange a certain mix of flowers to make a particular shape, remember to be bold in your decisions.

Flowers and houses

Although flowers are amazingly adaptable when it comes to combining them with other flowers and placing them around the house, the age and style of the building can substantially influence your style of flower arrangements. Contemporary houses, especially those with large plate glass windows and minimalist decorations, generally suggest simple and unfussy arrangements, maybe using only one type of flower, and possibly using just one colour as well. The containers, too, should be simple both in shape and form to create the best effect.

However, many of the houses now being built have a neo-Georgian character and these and their real Georgian forbears need more classical arrangements. That is not to say that these arrangements must be very formal, but they should show something of the elegance and refinement of that period. Likewise the containers need not be actual Georgian ones, but neither should they be stark modern sculptures.

As well as bearing in mind the period of the house, make sure that the proportions of the arrangement are suitable, so that it relates to the height of the ceiling and the room size. So in a well-proportioned Georgian town house, for example, you can afford to create more extravagant flower arrangements, which in a smaller modern house would look out of place. I always think that simple combinations of flowers look best, no matter what the setting; arrangements should always look natural and never appear to have been

*A*n abundant
arrangement in a blue
and white faience
cachepot stands before
a doorway into the
courtyard of Ightham
Mote in Kent. The
delphiniums pick up
the blue of the design
amidst a sea of white
dill, pale green
maidenhair fern, a
sprinkling of yellow
alstroemeria, and the
blossom-like stems of
tea tree.

**PLANT
—MATERIAL—
Delphiniums, dill,
maidenhair fern,
alstroemeria and tea
tree**

A squint opening on to Ightham Mote chapel (below) is a perfect place for this iridescent glass vase of arum lilies. The shape of these graceful flowers is echoed by the carved stone of the archway. In the hallway (right), a large arrangement of flowers in glowing pinks, lilacs and greens stands out boldly against the Tudor, black oak balustrading.

**PLANT
—MATERIAL—
Arum lilies**

**PLANT
—MATERIAL—
Lilies, Guelder roses, horse chestnut buds, lilac, snapdragons, camellias and bells of Ireland**

tortured into shape. With this in mind it follows that a simple jug arrangement can look equally at home in a contemporary or Georgian setting, but whereas one type of flower, such as yellow lilies or stems of lilac, would look best in the contemporary room, a mixture of simple country flowers and foliage would be better suited to the Georgian setting.

Ightham Mote in Kent

Stepping back into the past can be an illuminating experience and for some of us we do just that every time we go into our homes, which may date back to the Edwardian, Victorian, Regency or Georgian periods. Few of us live in houses that are older than this, though there are still houses surviving today that have been preserved and some are open to the public. Ightham Mote, owned by the National Trust, is one such house. It is an idyllic, "small" manor house standing in a Kent valley surrounded by a moat. It is easy to imagine the joy of living in such a house, for its

scale makes it extremely approachable in today's terms. Built around a central courtyard, the house is full of light and there are endless views through leaded windows to the gardens and rolling countryside beyond. When asked to decorate the interior of this house with flower arrangements, there was plenty of inspiration to be found, from its traditional, solid construction of stone and wood, to its old-style furnishings, plus, of course, the lovely country setting. Here, both informal country garden arrangements as well as the more stately displays look perfect, and even the most humble of arrangements using simple cottage garden flowers seem suitable.

In any type of building there will always be plenty to inspire beautiful flower creations, whether it is the mood and atmosphere of a house, the colour and texture of the wood and brickwork, or the garden or view outside. But if you are still unsure how to begin, look to the flowers themselves for inspiration and you won't go far wrong.

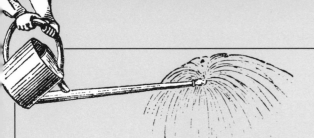

Essential information

There is not a great deal that you need to know about flowers, nor a great deal of equipment that you will require before you are able to create your own arrangements. However, there are a few guidelines you should follow if you want to keep your flowers in good condition so that they will last as long as possible once arranged. This section contains all the essential information you will need to know, from advice on preparing and caring for your plants, to more detailed instructions for wiring flowers and wrapping bouquets.

Once they are cut, flowers only live for a short time unless they are put into water, and once in water they need to be able to take up water easily to last well. To help this process, it is best to cut their stems at a very sharp angle with a pair of florists' or good kitchen scissors or a sharp knife. The angle is important because this exposes a large area of the inside of the stem, helping the flower to draw up the water more efficiently. You should always cut the stem, even if you have only recently picked the flowers in the garden, and certainly if you have bought the flowers from a flower shop. When the stem is soft it should be bruised as little as possible, so a sharp cut is best. Hard brown stems are a different matter – after cutting, these need to be hammered. Hollow stems should be cut and then filled with water and either plugged or upended with your thumb over the end, into the vase water, while stems containing milky sap should be sealed with a flame. Once the plant material has had a good drink of water for at least a couple of hours it is ready for arranging.

Hints on containers

The choice of container to arrange your flowers in is very personal, but if you want flowers to last as long as possible, shallow containers are best avoided. Many useful-sized containers can be adapted to look more attractive; for instance, a simple bucket can be covered with moss or hay before you use it for an arrangement. If the container is not very high or if it does not have an incurving lip, the flowers will need some support. Wet foam can be very useful for this purpose.

There are a few occasions when you will need to wire flowers before arranging them. Hollow but weak-stemmed flowers can have a wire pushed up their stem to strengthen them. This will also make them a little more pliable, but in general it should be the natural shape of the stem itself rather than an artificially produced shape that gives strength of form to an arrangement. However, flowers used in wedding bouquets and for wearing on clothes or in the hair often need to be completely wired so that they can be arranged into the exact design of your choice.

Finally, in this section, there are lots of helpful hints concerned with the finishing touches of making an attractive flower presentation, such as gift-wrapping a bouquet and making decorative bows.

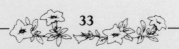

Tools and materials

To help you create successful flower arrangements, you need only a few essential tools and materials. Of primary importance are some good cutting implements: secateurs for thick, woody stems, florists' scissors for green stems and wire cutters.

You will need wires of various lengths and thicknesses to strengthen hollow stems for a grand arrangement, and to create stems and make them more pliable for complicated posy, garland and wreath work (see p.44). Reel wire is essential for tying together a wired bunch or bouquet. And you will need gutta-percha tape, raffia or ribbon to conceal wiring.

Foam is invaluable when creating container arrangements when the lip of the container will not support the stems of the flowers. A slab should be thoroughly wetted and then wedged into position in the vase or fixed to a florists' spike, itself stuck to the bottom of the container with adhesive clay (see p.38). You will then have no difficulty in securing the stems in the foam in precisely the positions you require. The foam is easily concealed with a layer of moss (also used for wreaths) and the whole can be topped up with water when necessary. Chicken-wire gives you less control but is useful for arrangements in incurving vases.

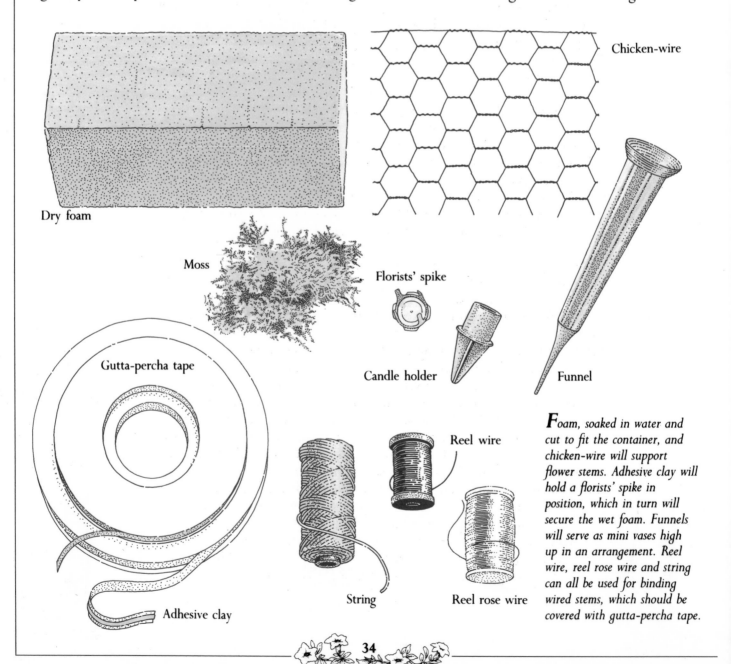

Chicken-wire

Dry foam

Moss

Florists' spike

Candle holder

Funnel

Gutta-percha tape

Reel wire

String

Reel rose wire

Adhesive clay

*F*oam, soaked in water and cut to fit the container, and chicken-wire will support flower stems. Adhesive clay will hold a florists' spike in position, which in turn will secure the wet foam. Funnels will serve as mini vases high up in an arrangement. Reel wire, reel rose wire and string can all be used for binding wired stems, which should be covered with gutta-percha tape.

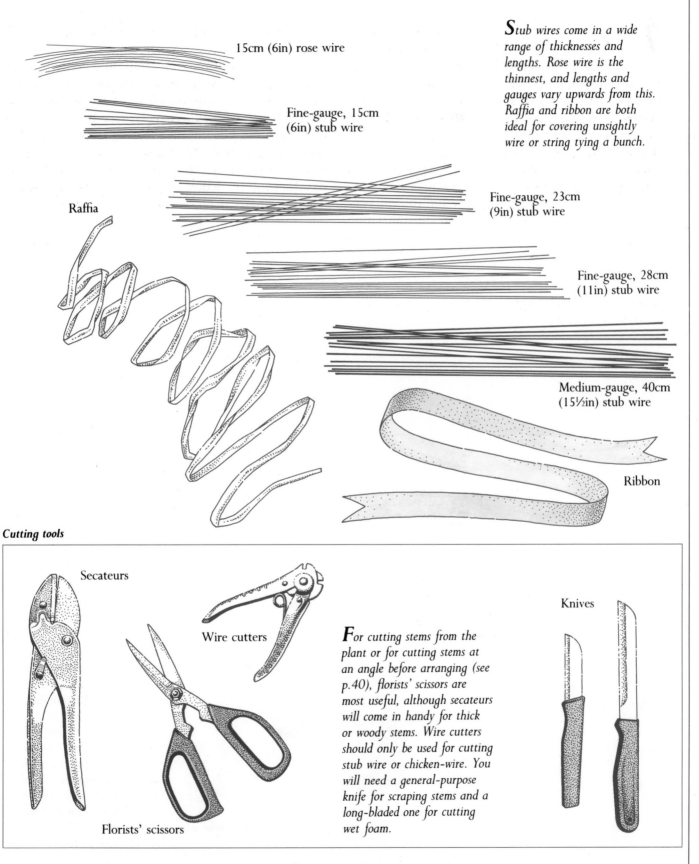

15cm (6in) rose wire

*S*tub wires come in a wide range of thicknesses and lengths. Rose wire is the thinnest, and lengths and gauges vary upwards from this. Raffia and ribbon are both ideal for covering unsightly wire or string tying a bunch.

Fine-gauge, 15cm (6in) stub wire

Raffia

Fine-gauge, 23cm (9in) stub wire

Fine-gauge, 28cm (11in) stub wire

Medium-gauge, 40cm (15½in) stub wire

Ribbon

Cutting tools

Secateurs

Wire cutters

Knives

*F*or cutting stems from the plant or for cutting stems at an angle before arranging (see p.40), florists' scissors are most useful, although secateurs will come in handy for thick or woody stems. Wire cutters should only be used for cutting stub wire or chicken-wire. You will need a general-purpose knife for scraping stems and a long-bladed one for cutting wet foam.

Florists' scissors

Suitable containers

There is an enormous variety of containers suitable for displaying fresh flowers, from the most ornately decorated, highly glazed, grand Victorian vase to the simplest, rustic-looking little basket. You will probably find that you already have masses of containers to choose from at home, for there is no reason to suppose that the only containers suitable are those that were made with flowers in mind. Tea cups, milk jugs, ink pots, tea caddies, shopping baskets, watering cans: all these useful receptacles and many more can be used to contain your fresh flower creations, always remembering to relate the shape and colours of each arrangement to that of the container.

If the stems of your flowers are in good condition, glass containers, such as the one on p.65, can show off your arrangement very effectively. Porous containers, such as baskets, boxes and unglazed terracotta pots or jugs, are often just right for informal, cottage-garden arrangements but these will need to be made waterproof first. To prepare one for fresh flowers, simply line it with plastic (see p.38) or other waterproof sheeting and conceal this with moss.

Glass containers
These range from enormous goldfish bowls to elegant single specimen and delicate, curvaceous opaque vases.

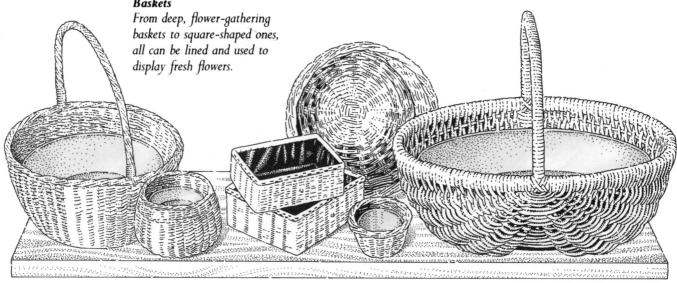

Baskets
From deep, flower-gathering baskets to square-shaped ones, all can be lined and used to display fresh flowers.

Ceramic containers
Some of the most sophisticated glazed vases and porcelain jugs are to be found in this group.

Terracotta containers
Warm and earthy-looking, terracotta and flowers look natural together.

Metal containers
Copper bowls and brass cachepots make good flower vases, as do metal caddies and even silver goblets and tankards.

—Preparing & adapting containers—

Although it is not necessary to prepare every single container for displaying fresh flowers – simpler, natural-looking arrangements can look stunning arranged nonchalantly in a jug of water (see p.229) – flower arranging is often much simpler if the stems are held in supporting material.

Wet foam (see p.34) is the most efficient supporting material. It is easy to sculpt and, if your container is especially large, you can always bind two pieces of wet foam together and fix both to the bottom on florists' spikes (see p.34). Make sure that the foam is thoroughly soaked. If you are preparing a glass vase with wet foam and you wish to conceal it, simply surround it with moss: it loves the water. If the vase has incurving sides, chicken-wire might be a good solution, and, for a simple arrangement, marbles or pebbles will hold flower stems in position as well as adding attractive and unusual decoration.

Some containers will definitely require lining before you fill them with water! Others will need adapting on the outside. An unsightly bucket can be covered prettily with hay; an ugly vase can be concealed by a knotted handkerchief, and a clear glass one decorated with colourful paper. You can also create a fresh flower wreath or circlet by following the instructions on the opposite page.

Preparing ceramic containers

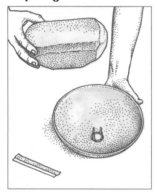

For an outcurving bowl, secure wet foam to a florists' spike fixed to the bottom of the bowl with adhesive clay.

For an incurving flower vase, stretch a piece of chicken-wire inside the rim until it grips the lipped sides.

Preparing glass containers

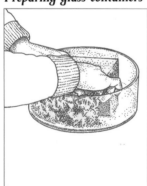

Fix two florists' spikes to the bottom of the container with adhesive clay. Sculpt a block of wet foam to fit neatly inside the container.

Secure the foam on to the florists' spikes in the centre of the vase. Surround and cover the foam with clumps of damp moss.

Lining porous containers

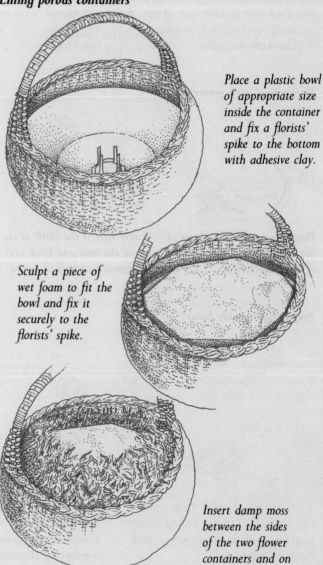

Place a plastic bowl of appropriate size inside the container and fix a florists' spike to the bottom with adhesive clay.

Sculpt a piece of wet foam to fit the bowl and fix it securely to the florists' spike.

Insert damp moss between the sides of the two flower containers and on top of the foam.

Adapting a bucket

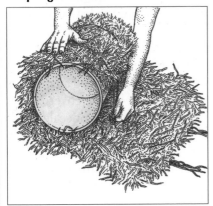

Place two strands of raffia on the floor, and cover with a thick layer of hay. Roll the bucket over the hay, holding the hay in place with the raffia.

Tie the ends of the raffia into bows, and add further ties if necessary to secure the hay in place. Trim any untidy pieces of hay with scissors.

Using marbles

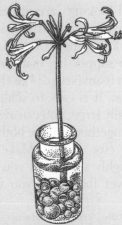

Coloured marbles, shells or pebbles will both secure stronger-stemmed material and make a small glass vase look all the more attractive.

Decorating with material

Place the vase in the centre of the cloth and tie knots in each of the four corners.

Gently stretch the cloth to the top of the vase and hitch over the knotted corners to secure.

Decorating with paper

Glue scraps of paper to the inside of the clear vase, overlapping the edges. Varnish to prevent the paper from peeling. Place a lining vase inside the decorated vase.

Preparing circular bases

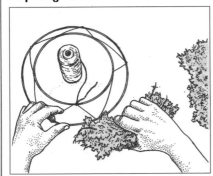

To a shop-bought wire frame, tie the end of a reel of string, leaving a short length beyond the knot. Take a small clump of damp moss.

Holding the moss against the frame, bind it on securely with the string. Continue binding around the frame, overlapping the clumps.

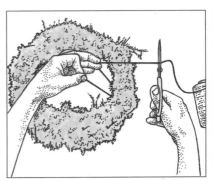

Overlap the last clump of moss with the first and bind it in. Cut the string and tie the end to the original knot end to make a neat finish.

Preparing plant material

Having prepared the container and collected the plant material, it is well worth pausing for just a few minutes to prepare the material. With a little attention at this stage the flowers will last longer and the arrangement look more attractive.

Even if you have only just cut the stems from the plant, you should always cut them anew at a sharp angle to expose a wider surface area. Next, strip all the lower leaves from the stems: otherwise they will only rot in the water. Scraping the bottom of green stems or hammering and cutting the bottom of woody stems helps them to take up water. Then stand all plant material in water for a couple of hours before arranging, pouring water into hollow stems first.

If the stems are reasonably robust, it is often a good idea to plunge them briefly into hot water to encourage them further to take up water. Some flowers can be revived by soaking them in or running them under cool water. Milky stems should be singed to prevent them from oozing in the vase. And the uppermost buds (which will never flower) of particularly buddy plants should be removed.

Cutting stems

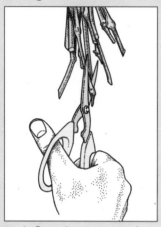

With florists' scissors, cut the stem at a sharp angle to expose a greater surface area to the water.

Stripping leaves

With your hand, strip the lower leaves from the stem to prevent them from rotting in the water.

Stripping branches

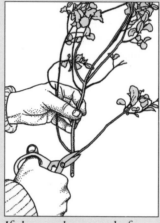

If the stem has many leafy branches, remove the lower ones with scissors, so no leaves sit in the water.

Stripping thorns

If the stem is thorny, it is a good idea to remove the thorns with scissors to make the stem easier to handle.

Scraping stems
With a knife or scissors scrape the lower end of the stem to encourage it to take up water quickly and efficiently.

Opening woody or brown stems

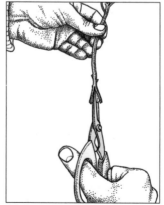

To encourage this tougher stem to take up water more efficiently, first hammer the end to split it.

With a pair of florists' scissors, make a cut in the base of the stem, about 2cm (¾in) up from the stem end.

Plants for this method
Beech, camellia, chestnut, Guelder rose, laurel, lilac, maple, oak, cedar, pine, rhododendron, most foliage plants

Filling hollow stems Method 1

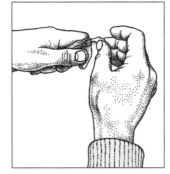

To ensure that water reaches the flower-head quickly, thus making it last longer, hold the stem upside-down and carefully pour water into it.

When the stem is full, plug the end with a small piece of wet cotton wool and place the stem in a vase of water immediately.

Plants for this method
Amaryllis, delphinium, hippeastrum, lupin

Filling hollow stems Method 2

Pour water into the stem as above, then place your thumb tightly over the end.

Upend the stem into a vase filled with water, preferably the one in which the arrangement will be made.

Singeing milky stems

Treating buddy stems

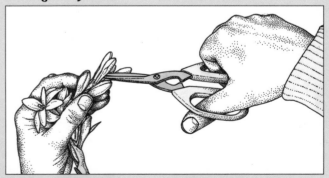

To seal an oozing stem, singe the cut end with the flame from a lighted match.

Plants for this method
Euphorbia, ferns, milkweed, poppy

To allow the buds lower down a long buddy stem to drink some water and therefore flower, remove the topmost buds (which will never flower) where the cut will not show with a pair of florists' scissors.

Plants for this method
Gladiolus, kaffir lily, tuberose

Plunging stems in hot water

Plants for this method
Alexanders, angelica, bamboo, bear's breeches, bistort, black-eyed Susan, butterfly bush, cock's comb, cow parsley, dogwood, gerbera, globe flower, hollyhock, laburnum, magnolia, mallow, sunflower, viper's bugloss, wormwood

Many stems will take up water even more quickly if plunged in hot water. Pour the water into the container, protecting the flowers from the steam. This hot water treatment will often revive flagging or wilting plant material.

Reviving flowers

Some flowers and most foliage can be revived by submerging them in cool water or running cool water over them.

Plants for this method
Heather, violet, most foliage

Straightening bendy stems

To make bendy-stemmed flowers easier to arrange, cut them, then wrap them in newspaper in bunches of four or five stems.

Secure each newspaper bunch with sticky tape, and place in a bucket of water. Leave overnight in a cool place, then use in an arrangement.

Plants for this method
Gerbera, rose, tulip

Caring for plant material

Cut flowers do not take a lot of looking after if they have been prepared appropriately. However, it is important not to place fresh flowers directly in front of a radiator, or in strong direct sunlight, as the heat will cause the flowers to droop remarkably quickly. Nor is it advisable to place an arrangement in a spot where people are always brushing against the flowers.

Adding a solution of bleach and sugar to the vase water will prolong the life of the plant material, and changing the water regularly helps to keep it fresh-smelling. Removing flower-heads as they die keeps the arrangement attractive-looking for longer.

Prolonging life

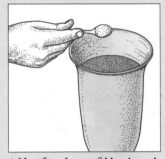 

Add a few drops of bleach and then a teaspoon of sugar to the vase water, and stir.

Alternatively, pour some flower crystals into the empty vase. Add a small amount of hot water and stir the solution to dissolve the crystals. Then top up the vase with cold tap water to the required level.

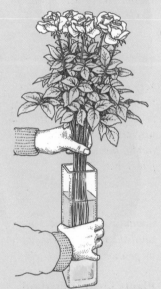

Changing the water
Replace the water in the vase frequently. Remove the whole bunch and put to one side. Pour out the water and replace with clean water.

Plants for this method
Godetia, stock, wallflower

Removing dead heads
Using your fingers or scissors, remove dead heads to ensure that the other flowers last well and that any new buds flower.

Wiring plant material

Wiring plant material is necessary only when an arrangement requires the flowers and foliage to be contorted into precisely the right position. Wedding posies, circlets and pew ends (see pp.196–205) make such a demand, as do complicated garlands (see p.213). Wiring the stems can serve both to strengthen them and to make them more pliable.

Hollow-stemmed material is simple to wire: insert a piece of wire into the centre, where it will not be visible. With other stems and leaves, wire must be bound around the outside, as shown on the following pages, and then covered with gutta-percha tape, so that no unsightly wire is visible.

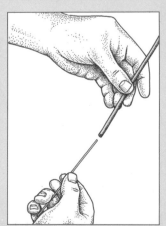

Wiring hollow stems
Take a piece of stub wire of appropriate length and gauge to fit neatly inside the stem, and insert the wire carefully to the top of the stem.

Plants for this method
Delphinium, hyacinth, larkspur, ranunculus

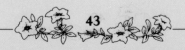

Wiring for wedding and other special arrangements

Method 1

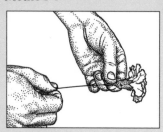

Push a stub wire up 1cm (½in) of the stem into the base of the flower.

Plants for this method
Rose, carnation, spray carnation, small lily, orchid

Method 2

Choose a stub wire of the right gauge to support the flower-head firmly. Cut the flower with 1cm (½in) of stalk and push the stub wire up the base. Bend the wire into a U shape.

Pull the wire back so that the U-shaped end returns back through the flower. Squeeze the ends together.

Plants for this method
Single chrysanthemum, everlasting flower, marigold, single rose

Method 4

This method is a little more difficult than the preceding ones. First push a fine rose wire carefully through the base of the flower.

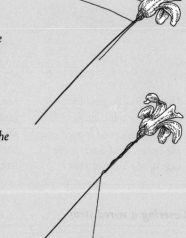

Next push a stub wire of a gauge to hold the flower into the flower base. Bend the shorter end of wire down beside it.

Very gently but firmly bend the other end of the rose wire in a spiral down over the stub wire and its other end. Be careful not to damage the flower base.

Continue twisting the wire until the flower is held firmly in position.

Plants for this method
Stephanotis, hyacinth, single nerine, single freesia

Method 3

Cut the flower with 2.5cm (1in) of stem. Place a stub wire against the stem and a fine rose wire against this, so the wire protrudes upwards.

Bend the longer rose wire end down and begin to spiral it tightly around the stalk and stub wire to hold the stem firmly in place.

Twist the rose wire round the stub wire to complete the wiring.

Plants for this method
Flowers with thin stems such as freesia, small groups of flowers

Wiring lily-of-the-valley

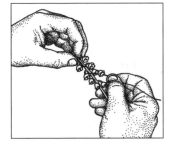

Make a 5mm (¹/₈in) U with the end of a fine rose wire. Hook it near the top of the flower stem with the end running down parallel to the spire of flowers.

Very gently twist the rose wire round the stem of the flowers between each single flower. Be very careful not to break the stem.

Continue to wind the rose wire down the stem. Then wire as in method 3.

Plants for this method
Lily-of-the-valley, small trails of ivy leaves

Wiring single leaves

Using fine- or medium-gauge rose wire, make a hair pin with one end longer than the other, and insert either side of the central vein.

Hook the wire through the leaf. Place a stub wire by the stem. Twist the longer end of the rose wire around stem, stub wire and itself.

Twist the wire until the leaf is held firmly.

Plants for this method
Italian arum, camellia

Covering a wired stem

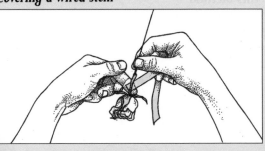

Holding the wired flower-head downwards, place a piece of gutta-percha tape, the same length as the stub wire, at an angle against the top of the wired stem.

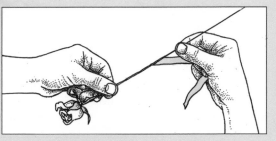

Holding the gutta-percha tape so it is stretched taut, revolve the wired stem so that the tape covers itself in a spiral up the wire. Twist to seal the tape at the top of the wire.

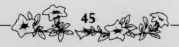

—Wrapping & decorating bouquets—

A bouquet, however simple, makes a lovely present, but, as with most gifts, the packaging counts for a lot. You can create a perfect and sumptuous bouquet arrangement (see p.54 for an idea), using a simply stunning array of beautiful flowers, or a collection of flowers specially chosen for their significant meanings, but without the stylish wrapping or the complementary bow, the bouquet will not look complete and will probably not give as much joy as it ought.

Wrapping a bouquet is not a difficult matter. Choose paper in colours and patterns that both complement the flowers and that you know the recipient will like. Alternatively, wrap the flowers in cellophane, so that the flowers are visible in all their glory. Try to wrap the flowers only a short time before you present them as they will soon wilt out of water.

However you wrap the flowers, make sure that you adorn the bouquet with either colourful ribbons – for a bright, joyous, perhaps sophisticated look – or raffia – for a more rustic effect. The effect of the bow or bows should be dramatic yet in keeping with the style of the bouquet and the colours of the flowers. You can either stick to using single bows for simplicity, or make a multiple bow with several brightly coloured ribbons. To complete the bow, leave the long ribbon-ends to trail and curl decoratively down the bouquet.

Wrapping bouquets with paper

 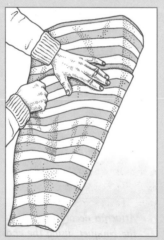  

Spread the wrapping paper face-down on a table. Place the bouquet across the top at an angle and draw the top left-hand corner over the flowers.

Take hold of the corner diagonally opposite and bring the rest of the wrapping paper up and over the top of the first corner.

Slide the paper under the flowers and secure with sticky tape. Fold the point back at the bottom of the bouquet and secure with sticky tape.

Fold over the broad triangle at the top of the bouquet to protect the flowers, and secure it carefully and discreetly with sticky tape.

Making single bows

Take a good length of ribbon from the reel and make a loop, leaving a generous amount over.

Holding the ribbon at the cross-over point, make another loop to create a figure-of-eight.

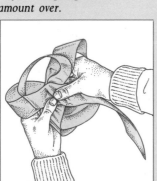

Make two more loops in the same way to pivot on the central point, and cut the ribbon at an angle.

At the back of the bow, pleat the ribbon at the cross-over point to bring the centre of the ribbon together.

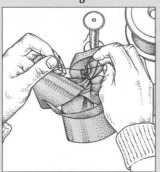

Wind reel wire several times around the pleated centre of the ribbon to secure the bow. Knot and cut the wire.

Cut away the ends of the wire and pull out the loops. The bow is now ready to tie to a bouquet of flowers.

Completing cellophane bouquets

Wrap with cellophane in the same way as paper. Secure by tying narrow ribbon around the stems.

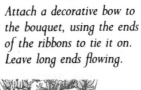

Attach a decorative bow to the bouquet, using the ends of the ribbons to tie it on. Leave long ends flowing.

Draw the blunt edge of a knife or scissors along the lengths of ribbon to make them wavy.

Making multiple bows

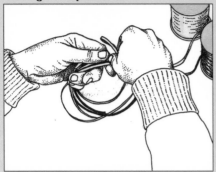

Take two narrow or string ribbons of contrasting or complementary colours and loop them together around the fingers of one hand to create at least six circles, one on top of the other.

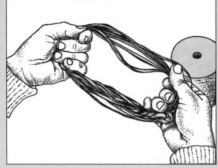

Cut the ribbon from the reel with a pair of scissors. Then, using both hands, grasp the multi-ribboned circle at opposite sides and slowly and carefully draw it out to form a long oval shape.

Twist one end over to form a figure-of-eight.

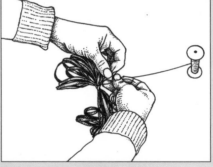

Wind reel wire around the cross-over point to secure. Cut the wire and tie a small knot at the back of the multiple bow. Pull out and neaten the loops.

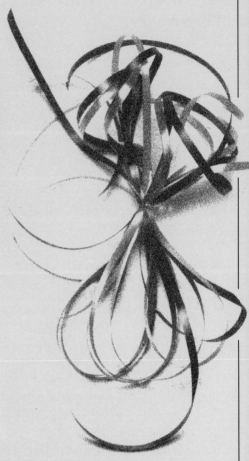

Making raffia bows

Before making the bow, tie the stems together using one strand of raffia, and knot.

Take two more strands of raffia and loop them twice.

Holding the centre, pull out the loops into a figure-of-eight.

Tie the raffia bow to the bouquet, using the raffia that is binding the stems.

Cut the ends of the tying raffia to the length required and tease out the loops.

Useful tips

Choosing flowers to combine in an arrangement is often just as exciting as the actual arranging, but it can be useful to know whether the flowers are all going to last well. To help you in your choice of flowers, below are some lists of long-lived flowers and foliage, together with some short-lived ones.

If your passion is for wild flowers, however, it would be as well to take note of the list of protected plants (right), the picking of any of which can result in a fine of up to £500 for each plant. It is always best to grow wild flowers that you like in your own garden.

Finally, I have also put together some of my favourite combinations of flowers that I particularly enjoy using when creating arrangements.

—LONG-LASTING FLOWERS—

Amaryllis	Globe thistle
Bear's breeches	Golden rod
Bird of paradise flower	Masterwort
Camellia	Michaelmas daisy
Cape cowslip	Painter's palette
Carnation	Peruvian lily
China aster	Protea
Chincherinchee	Sea holly
Chrysanthemum	Slipper orchid
Cupid's dart	Statice
Cymbidium	Sword lily
Gayfeather	Yarrow

—LONG-LASTING FOLIAGE— / —SHORT-LIVED FLOWERS—

Banksia	African lily
Box	Astilbe
Butcher's broom	Bergamot
Camellia foliage	Butterfly bush
Fan palm	Gentian
Grevillea	Hibiscus
Griselinia	Laburnum
Holly	Lenten rose
Ivy	Mimosa
Juniper	Poppy
Pine	Sweet pea
Rhododendron foliage	Violet
Skimmia	Zinnia
Spotted laurel	
Spruce	
Yew	

—FAVOURITE COMBINATIONS—

Mixed old-fashioned roses. Camellia, lilac and ranunculus.
Cow parsley, paeonies and snapdragons.
Delphiniums and foxgloves. Lilies and nerines.
Guelder roses, mock orange and flowering whitebeam.
Red hot pokers, montbretia and yarrow.
Wintersweet, witch hazel and winter honeysuckle.

—PROTECTED PLANTS—

Adder's tongue spearwort
Ranunculus ophioglossifolius
Alpine catchfly
Lychnis alpina
Alpine gentian
Gentiana nivalis
Alpine woodsia
Woodsia alpina
Bedstraw broomrape
Orobanche caryophyllacea
Blue heath
Phyllodoce caerulea
Brown galingale
Cyperus fuscus
Cheddar pink
Dianthus gratianopolitanus
Childling pink
Petrorhagia nanteuilii
Diapensia
Diapensia lapponica
Dickie's bladder-fern
Cystopteris dickieana
Downy woundwort
Stachys germanica
Drooping saxifrage
Saxifraga cernua
Early spider-orchid
Ophrys sphegodes
Fen orchid
Liparis loeselii
Fen violet
Viola persicifolia
Field cow-wheat
Melampyrum arvense
Field eryngo
Eryngium campestre
Field wormwood
Artemisia campestris
Ghost orchid
Epipogium aphyllum
Greater yellow-rattle
Rhinanthus serotinus
Jersey cudweed
Gnaphalium luteoalbum
Lady's-slipper
Cypripedium calceolus
Late spider-orchid
Ophrys fuciflora
Least lettuce
Lactuca saligna
Limestone woundwort
Stachys alpina
Lizard orchid
Himantoglossum hircinum
Military orchid
Orchis militaris
Monkey orchid

Orchis simia
Norwegian sandwort
Arenaria norvegica
Oblong woodsia
Woodsia ilvensis
Oxtongue broomrape
Orobanche loricata
Perennial knawel
Scleranthus perennis
Plymouth pear
Pyrus cordata
Purple spurge
Euphorbia peplis
Red helleborine
Cephalanthera rubra
Ribbon-leaved water-plantain
Alisma gramineum
Rock cinquefoil
Potentilla rupestris
Rock sea-lavender
Limonium paradoxum
Rough marsh-mallow
Althaea hirsuta
Sea knotgrass
Polygonum maritimum
Sickle-leaved hare's-ear
Bupleurum falcatum
Small alison
Alyssum alyssoides
Small hare's-ear
Bupleurum baldense
Snowdon lily
Lloydia serotina
Spiked speedwell
Veronica spicata
Spring gentian
Gentiana verna
Starfruit
Damasonium alisma
Starved wood-sedge
Carex depauperata
Teesdale sandwort
Minuartia stricta
Thistle broomrape
Orobanche reticulata
Triangular club-rush
Scirpus triquetrus
Tufted saxifrage
Saxifraga cespitosa
Water germander
Teucrium scordium
Whorled solomon's seal
Polygonatum verticillatum
Wild gladiolus
Gladiolus illyricus
Wood calamint
Calamintha sylvatica

Making the most of flowers

There is no need to find the thought of creating an arrangement of flowers daunting. Although there are no hard and fast rules about what will look attractive in an arrangement, there are some guidelines – demonstrated in this section – that you may find useful for creating an enormous range of arrangements, from a bunch of flowers made into a bouquet or posy to give as a present, to a centrepiece for the dining table for a dinner party, or even larger arrangements, to stand on a hall table or on the hearth of a fireplace. Whichever type of arrangement you wish to make, it is simply a matter of choosing a group of flowers with interesting flower shapes and foliage that go together well, and whose colours work with the decoration of the room in which the arrangement will be placed. Scent, too, is another important consideration.

These factors are not nearly as restricting as they may at first sound. Flowers are so beautiful that almost any combination of forms and colours is bound to look attractive, so you start with a great advantage. As long as one of the main colours in the flower arrangement complements the colour of the walls, carpets or curtains, the whole display will probably look absolutely meant for the position that you have chosen. The scale of an arrangement is important, especially if it is for a special occasion at which a large group of people will be present. Then the flowers must be arranged so that they will be seen to their best advantage. It is surprising how even the tiniest vase of flowers sitting on a side table or window ledge will attract attention. Do not restrict yourself to flowers and foliage – try combining them with fruit and vegetables, or mixing them with pot plants; above all be adventurous. On the following pages you will find flowers arranged in many different ways, which I hope will act as a starting point for you to create your own arrangements.

THE ART OF COMPOSITION

Some people worry much too much about arranging flowers. There is absolutely no need for anxiety. Flowers are so beautiful with such exciting shapes, colours and textures that you cannot go far wrong when arranging them. The way that they grow usually gives a good insight into how they will look best when arranged. But here are a few guidelines on composing arrangements for those needing some extra courage before starting.

The simplest kind of flower arrangement is the bunch. There are two sorts of "arranged" bunches: the posy, in which the flowers are arranged in a circular fashion, to be seen from all round; and the bouquet, in which the flowers are set out in a fan shape and designed to be seen only from the front. The disadvantage with bunches is that they soon wilt. However, it is often possible to place a posy or bouquet into a vase of water without rearranging the flowers at all. Simply remove the wrapping and ties and cut the stems at a sharp angle.

Arrangements in containers

By arranging posies and bouquets in vases you can create two of the simplest forms of container arrangement. From a posy you can make an all-round arrangement ideal for an occasional table, and from a bouquet you can make a flat-backed arrangement suitable for standing against a wall or mirror.

When starting from scratch, a fan shape is the easiest to create. If the arrangement will be seen from all sides, then it should have the outline of a fan wherever it is viewed. A flat-backed arrangement will look like an open fan from the front and a half-closed fan from the sides.

Choose containers that relate not only to the flowers but to the surrounding decorations. As a rough guide, the container should be one-third of the total height of the arrangement and container combined and half the total width. When arranging flowers, create generous curves and strong lines, allowing the plant material to accentuate these shapes naturally. Never let the arrangement become too evenly spaced, or it will look unnatural.

A sense of place

The scale of an arrangement must relate to the space in which it stands. Dinner tables and coffee tables require low all-round arrangements, whereas hall side tables usually demand tall, flat-backed arrangements.

When deciding on the flowers to use in an arrangement, consider not only the space it is to occupy but also the colours of the surrounding walls and furnishings. I do not like flowers to match the decorations too slavishly as the arrangement tends to look too contrived. For safety choose just one colour or a combination of colours that are not too far apart in the colour spectrum or a range of pastel colours. For a more exciting effect, incorporate a small quantity of bright colours with an otherwise pastel creation.

That special touch

Scent is a major consideration when arranging flowers. Scented flowers make any arrangement just that bit more special and it is lovely to have a room smelling sweetly of flowers. Placing bowls of your own specially mixed pot pourri in your rooms is another way of adding perfume to your surroundings.

Nature can show you the way to make interesting arrangements. Here, twisting-stemmed poppies look as if they are growing amongst the little white daisies in this shallow, deep red glass dish.

—PLANT MATERIAL—
Iceland poppies and daisies

Bouquets

Whether they contain one sort of flower or a pretty mix of flowers and foliage, bouquets are usually simple to make and always a pleasure to receive. A bouquet is the perfect gift to take to a friend who has invited you for lunch or dinner, or for a neighbour who is ill or who has done you a favour. A bouquet also makes a lovely birthday or anniversary gift, especially if the flowers chosen convey a special meaning (see p.194).

Although many bouquets are easy to make, it is important not simply to bunch together any flowers that happen to be to hand. Consider carefully your choice of flowers, making sure that the colours combine happily. Why not include some scented flowers?

Freesias, pinks and sweet-smelling roses can all look lovely in bouquets. If you have none to pick in your garden, you can always buy them from your local flower shop. And try to use some unusual forms and textures when combining several sorts of flower and foliage in your bouquet.

A bouquet can be any size you choose, ranging from a small bouquet of freesias and gypsophila or one composed of pinks and some silvery foliage, to a much grander bouquet of lilies, spray carnations and single spray chrysanthemums. Let the character of the recipient and the nature of the occasion be your guide.

—PLANT MATERIAL—
Single chrysanthemums,
carnations,
gerbera, Peruvian lilies,
gypsophila,
kerria foliage
and fern fronds

1

Begin to create this fan-shaped bouquet with three fronds of fern, the tallest in the centre. Set two single chrysanthemums on top of the middle fern so that the flower-heads sit just below the top of it. Place slightly shorter-stemmed Peruvian lilies on either side of the single chrysanthemums.

Bouquets have long been considered the perfect present for a lover to give, as this illustration from The Shepherd's Calendar *shows.*

2

Keeping the longest stems roughly at the centre of the bouquet, add some of the larger-flowered gerbera, the carnations and the kerria foliage. Make sure the shape is even. Place a layer of light, airy gypsophila over and around the flowers.

3

Continue layering the flowers, offsetting the shapes, colours and textures as you work down the bouquet. Where the stems overlap – about $\frac{1}{6}$th of the way up – tie a narrow ribbon, and attach a complementary bow (see p.46).

All-round arrangements

Whether circular or oval, low and simple or very tall and complicated, all-round arrangements look equally good from any angle. They are particularly suitable for free-standing tables such as dining tables or coffee tables, or for any location where the vase is not positioned close to a wall.

The best containers for all-round creations are the cylindrical and round-topped ones. Square and wide, elliptic and rectangular containers can also be suitable, and can vary from very low to quite tall vessels. Narrow vases are not so well suited to this type of arrangement and are much more effective when used for one-sided, or facing arrangements. However, most baskets, jugs and mugs are appropriate for all-round

arrangements, as are most materials: ceramic, glass, wicker, wood, metal or stone.

The correct height of an all-round arrangement depends on its situation. For instance, a low arrangement is best in the centre of a dining table, so that it does not block the view of one guest and his opposite number across the table. However, for a wide side table or to divide a room, a much taller all-round arrangement will be most attractive.

I like this type of arrangement most of all. It is lovely to be able to see through to the flowers and foliage at the back. Flat, one-sided arrangements look at their best when they are placed against a wall or in front of a mirror.

In this low, all-round arrangement, the flowers are only a few inches higher than the container and just slightly mounded. Because the stems are cut short, the arrangement will last well.

**PLANT
—MATERIAL—
Fruiting ivy, spray
roses, clove
carnations and
Iceland poppies**

Fruiting ivy
Hedera helix

1_____
Line a basket with plastic and fix a prong to the bottom with adhesive clay. Press a slightly rounded wedge of wet foam firmly on to the prong.

2_____
Insert stems of fruiting ivy firmly into the foam to make a low dome shape. Arrange some of the stems so that they hang down over the sides of the basket.

*A group of poppies with
decorative blotched centres.*

3

*Add roses randomly over the
mound. Follow these with
clove carnations and poppies.
Let some of the poppies fall
down against the sides of the
basket for a natural look.*

Spray rose
Rosa 'Dorus Rijkers'

Iceland poppy
Papaver nudicaule

Clove carnation
Dianthus 'Perfect Clove'

*P*erfectly proportioned and pretty, this all-round basket arrangement would make an ideal centrepiece on a country dining table.

—PLANT MATERIAL—
Eucalyptus, spray carnations, pink orchids, pink larkspur, prairie gentians and godetias

If your basket has a tall handle, try twining some foliage around it for a little extra decoration.

1
Fix a plastic prong to the bottom of a plastic container with adhesive clay. Place the container in the basket and secure a piece of well-soaked florists' foam on to the prong.

Fine-leaved eucalyptus
Eucalyptus pauciflora nana

Spray carnation
Dianthus 'Eolo'

2
Make the basic all-round curve shape with the eucalyptus: the stems should appear to spring from the lower centre of the arrangement and should rise slightly above the handle of the basket. Add the carnations informally, keeping the curve in proportion. Turn the arrangement as you work.

58

3

Following the line of the curve carefully, add the ice-pink larkspur. Next, add the orchids, the delicately arching stems of Eustoma grandiflorum *and the deep red godetias. Stand back and reassess the whole of the arrangement, adding ingredients to fill out the shape. Top up with water to ensure that the flowers last as long as possible.*

Ice-pink larkspur
Delphinium consolida

Bright pink orchid
Dendrobium nobile

Prairie gentian
Eustoma grandiflorum

Godetia
Clarkia 'Crimson Glow'

*E*legant and eye-catching, this tall, all-round arrangement would enliven many a sombre living-room. The vase is almost half the total height, so the stems of the plant material are kept long. Stability is often a problem with tall flower arrangements and it is sometimes best to secure the stems in wet foam or use chicken-wire to hold the arrangement together.

—PLANT MATERIAL—
Snowberries, Peruvian lilies, shining euphorbia and lilies

1
The incurving rim of this ceramic vase brings together the long stems.

2
With the foliage, form a strongly curving dome shape with the tallest stems at the centre. Add the snowberries and Peruvian lilies next, keeping the curve. Turn the vase as you work.

Snowberry
Symphoricarpos albus

Peruvian lily
Alstroemeria ligtu hybrid

Shining euphorbia
Euphorbia fulgens

3

Add the remainder of the
flowers, making sure that the
stems curve outwards from the
base of the pot. Keep the
overall shape informal for a
natural-looking effect.

Lily
Lilium 'Everest'

The first steps in the art of flower
arranging are being given in this
illustration from the Girl's Own Paper.

Facing arrangements

Flower arrangements are often placed against a wall where the back of the arrangement cannot be seen. These are known as facing, or flat-backed, arrangements, and for them to work successfully, it should appear as though they are really all-round arrangements when seen from either the front or the sides. It is never attractive for these flat-backed arrangements to be placed *directly* against the wall, unless it is absolutely necessary because of restricted space, as they can easily lose their three-dimensional feel if they are too narrow.

Flat-backed arrangements do, of course, save on the number of flowers needed, as you are only looking at the display from one side. The flowers at the sides of the altar can be displayed in a facing arrangement, thus saving on material. So, too, can a flower arrangement for a mantelpiece, a hall table, or a floor-standing arrangement for the corner of a room. However, the smaller the arrangement becomes, or the closer to the ground that it is to stand, the more unlikely it is that you will be able to use a flat-backed arrangement, as the back will be visible.

To arrange a flat-backed flower display, it is easiest to start with foliage first. Place this at the back of the arrangement, in a rough fan shape, level with the back of the vase. Then fill in with more foliage towards the front, before finally adding the flowers that you have decided to use.

Low, flat-backed flower arrangements work best when the back is not visible. This arrangement is displayed on a shelf at eye level.

—PLANT MATERIAL—
Camellia leaves, emerald feather, cream freesias, cream miniature orchids, pale pink roses, Peruvian lilies and pink broom

1

Fill the container with wet foam. Then arrange the foliage in a fan shape at the back of the container. Use the remainder of the greenery to fill in space towards the front.

Camellia leaves
Camellia cv.

Emerald feather
Asparagus densiflorus
'Sprengeri'

2

Cut the orchid stems into two sections, and place these with the cream freesias in the wet foam, following the shape of the foliage.

Cream miniature orchid
Dendrobium cv.

Cream freesia
Freesia × kewensis

3

Finally add the roses, broom and Peruvian lilies. The stems of Peruvian lilies can be split into five or six pieces, and as these are the most delicate it is best to insert them last.

Pale pink rose
Rosa cv.

Peruvian lily
Alstroemeria ligtu hybrid

Pink broom
Cytisus cv.

*T*his well-proportioned, flat-backed, or "facing", flower arrangement has been designed to sit against a wall, so the simple, straight-sided glass container is ideal. For such an arrangement, the fan-shaped network of foliage and flowers should be twice the height of the container and no more than three times the width.

White poplar
Populus alba

—PLANT MATERIAL—
Stems of white poplar, bells of Ireland, montbretia, pink roses, statice and phlox

Bells of Ireland
Moluccella laevis

Montbretia
Crocosmia masonorum

Pink rose
Rosa 'Bridal Pink'

1
Place the tallest stems of foliage in the centre and set curving stems to left and right and forwards. Do not let any material curve backwards.

Statice
Limonium sinuatum

Phlox
Phlox paniculata
'Rembrandt'

2
Now add the flowers one variety at a time. Ensure that you maintain an informal balance in the whole flat-backed, fan-shaped or semi-circular arrangement.

65

It is important to remember that arrangements which are to stand against a wall are usually seen from three sides, so the sides need as much attention as the front. Here, this tall, flat-backed arrangement displays eye-catching gerberas at the front and softer, pink-coloured chrysanthemums at the sides.

—PLANT MATERIAL—
Mexican orange blossom foliage, chrysanthemums, gerberas and tree heath

1 _____
Arrange the foliage in the vase in a roughly semi-circular shape. Carefully insert the chrysanthemums throughout the foliage.

Mexican orange blossom foliage
Choisya ternata

Gerbera
Gerbera cv.

Chrysanthemums
Chrysanthemum cv.

Tree heath
Erica terminalis

2

Position all the remaining flowers in the vase, making sure that the arrangement is filled at the sides as well as at the front.

This glorious flat-backed arrangement of paeonies, tulips, lilies and grasses shows off its decorated vase to great advantage.

Grand arrangements

*L*arge-scale arrangements are often created for special occasions where a large number of people are expected and the flower arrangements must be both tall and wide in order to be seen. They are often made to display on a pedestal in a church or reception.

A grand arrangement is one that stands at least 90cm (3ft) tall. Although it is possible to cut foliage this long, the stems of flowers are frequently substantially shorter than this. To overcome this problem, short-stemmed material is placed in funnel-like tubes, which are filled with water. The tubes are either inserted in the foam or wire base in the vase or, for even greater height, attached to lengths of cane, which are then fixed in the foam.

Most large arrangements are fan-shaped, although this depends entirely on how many sides the arrangement will be viewed. If, as is often the case, the arrangement is to be set against a wall, it will need to be flat-backed. If, however, the arrangement is to be placed near the pulpit or the main doors of a church, it may well need to be an all-round arrangement.

The scale of an arrangement should always be in keeping with the scale of the building. So, for a large space in a large building, where the flowers will be seen from afar, the plant material used in an arrangement should be bold: strong-shaped leaves and vibrant-coloured flowers are essential if you wish your creation to make a significant impact.

—PLANT MATERIAL—
Berberis, sweet chestnut leaves, fennel, larkspur, yellow roses, montbretia, Michaelmas daisies and pink lilies

To make this grand, majestic arrangement, *first cover a bucket with hay (see p.39). Next, pack wet foam into the bucket and insert three tubes into the foam. Arrange the long-stemmed foliage directly in the foam to make a fan shape. Follow this with the taller-stemmed flowers. Finally, pack the shorter-stemmed flowers, together with some foliage, in the tubes to provide eye-catching height.*

Bucket, hay, raffia, wet foam and three funnels

Berberis
Berberis thunbergii atropurpurea

Fennel
Foeniculum vulgare

Sweet chestnut
Castanea sativa

Michaelmas daisy
Aster novae-angliae

Larkspur
Delphinium ajacis

Yellow rose *Rosa*
'Golden Times'

Pink lily
Lilium speciosum
'Uchida'

Montbretia
Crocosmia masonorum

*S*een from three sides, this church pedestal arrangement includes bright- and pale-coloured flowers, so that it stands out in the dark interior of the church. Care was taken to ensure that the flowers did not obscure the altar.

The garland of laurel leaves lends this plinth and urn a classical air.

Bottlebrush foliage
Callistemon brachyandrus

*T*his all-round, floor-standing arrangement is on a large scale, requiring a lot of plant material. Tubes are essential to hold the shorter-stemmed flowers and foliage, and to add even more height to the already tall arrangement.

—PLANT MATERIAL—
Mexican orange blossom foliage, bottlebrush foliage, white roses, statice, chrysanthemums and delphiniums

Mexican orange blossom foliage
Choisya ternata

1
Line a terracotta pot with polythene, wedging it in place with wet foam. Form the structure of the arrangement by making a fan shape of tall foliage. Next, fix three tubes — the central one wired to a cane for extra height — from the centre to the back of the arrangement.

Chrysanthemum
Chrysanthemum 'Tokyo'

Chrysanthemum
Chrysanthemum 'Tuneful'

White rose
Rosa cv.

Statice
Limonium sinuatum

Delphinium
Delphinium Belladonna hybrid

Tube wired to length of cane

This ornate, handled urn calls for a splendid arrangement.

2

Fill out the shape with more foliage and the rigid stems of chrysanthemums. Next, add the delphiniums, and finally position the roses and statice directly into the foam and also into the tubes.

71

Arranging bunches

*I*t is surprising how different the same bunch of flowers can look when arranged with different types of foliage. Not only will the foliage determine the size of the arrangement, but it will also affect the colour of the flowers. Silver-coloured foliage softens and lightens the flowers, while dark green leaves serve to enhance and offset them.

The colour of the foliage will also suggest which type of container you should use. Dark evergreen leaves look best against a darker container, such as a rustic twig basket, whereas silvery foliage looks particularly attractive in a pale white or grey vase. In these flower arrangements, pink spray carnations are displayed with different types of foliage.

—PLANT MATERIAL—
Pink spray carnations, eucalyptus foliage, shallon foliage, fruiting ivy and gypsophila

Pink spray carnations are complemented here by silvery eucalyptus foliage in a whitewashed wicker basket.

The bright green leaves of shallon fall naturally into an attractive shape in this slim jug, and strongly enhance the carnation blooms.

Many varieties of carnation have been developed; the striped ones are particularly beautiful.

This low mound arrangement combines different textures. Delicate carnation blooms nestle amongst dark berries and leaves of fruiting ivy in a twiggy basket.

A soft mist of gypsophila makes an excellent substitute for foliage. This arrangement seems to froth out of the trumpet-shaped vase.

73

A bouquet of long-stemmed red roses looks wonderful in its pretty gift wrapping, but once the wrapping is removed, how can you display it if you have no other cut flowers available? On these pages are a few suggestions for displaying a bouquet of red roses — either together or separately — using only their own foliage for greenery and interest.

Old-fashioned roses make a traditional-looking bouquet.

—PLANT MATERIAL—
A bouquet of red roses

A shallow bowl of deep red roses can look wonderful on a low table. Here they nestle against one another, framed by their leaves, in a bowl that usually contains pot pourri.

This group of three cylindrical glass vases shows off all the roses to perfection, just as they appeared in the bouquet. The vases could equally well be displayed separately around the house.

A conical vase is an ideal shape for this more traditional all-round arrangement, which uses all the roses. The tallest stem is placed in the centre and the shorter stems on either side of it.

This low, mossy basket of roses would make an ideal small rustic table centrepiece. The gently rounded curves of the rose petals are set off by the foliage, which was taken from lower down the stems.

Single specimen vases were considered suitable for the dinner table in Cassell's Book of the Household *(1895)*.

*T*ulips are excellent cut flowers, and are extremely versatile in arrangements. Left on their own, the stems curve to make interesting shapes. Alternatively, you can straighten the stems by wrapping them in newspaper, then plunging them up to their necks in water and leaving them overnight.

An elegant blue and white tulip vase is used for this display of pink tulips that often have several buds on each stem. The stems curve within the arrangement.

These striking, red parrot tulips have an old-fashioned cottage look about them, and seem ideally suited to an arrangement in a twiggy basket. The container inside the basket must be kept well filled with water.

The contrast between the pink of the Attila tulips and the blue of the flower bowl gives this low arrangement dramatic interest. The stems have been cut short to keep the tulips compact and bushy.

76

Tulipa suaveolens

These floppy parrot tulips can be unwieldy to arrange in some containers, but in this low, glass vase they droop gracefully and look stunning.

A mixed posy or informal bouquet makes a perfect present for a special occasion, especially if some of the flowers are sweetly scented. It is often a simple matter to arrange such a bunch. Either place the bouquet straight in a vase, or arrange the flowers separately, perhaps dividing them by colour.

This delicate mix of daisies and corn would make a lovely informal, rustic-looking arrangement.

—PLANT MATERIAL—
Peach roses, cream freesias, pink cornflowers, variegated privet and eucalyptus

When the posy is laid open *on its side, the flowers almost arrange themselves into this narrow, pretty oval glass vase.*

A glowing yellow and gold arrangement is created (right) by using just the yellow freesias and privet. The remainder of the posy — the pink flowers and silver foliage — stand out well in the silver and turquoise vase (below).

ACCENT ON COLOUR

From day to day we do not take a great deal of notice of the colours that surround us: the trees and hedgerows, the walls in the rooms in which we live, or the fruit and vegetables at the greengrocers. We notice colour only occasionally, perhaps when we come to decorate or furnish a room, or when we dress for a special event. We should become more conscious of colour, and what better tutor than flowers? They grow in the most extraordinary array of colours. Some flowers, like godetia and phlox, have both loud and demure varieties – the most shocking pinks and the palest, softest pinks imaginable. There are the intense blues of delphiniums, the rich crimsons of roses and the greens and rusts of orchids. Every page of a plant encyclopedia overflows with colours, and they are all just waiting for us to use them in arrangements.

The theory of colour

There are no hard and fast rules that govern the use of colour in arrangements, but the colour spectrum offers some guidance. There are three primary colours in the colour spectrum – red, yellow and blue – and different combinations of these make the secondary colours – orange, green and purple. Varying shades and tones of all these colours are created by mixing them with white, the colour of light, or black, the colour of darkness.

The closer together colours are in the spectrum, the more likely they are to mix easily. This is all very well but a bit boring when it comes to flower arranging. Close colour combinations lack drama and there should be at least a little tingle of excitement in every flower arrangement.

In truth, most flower colours mix with ease and it is more a question of knowing *how much* of each colour to include to make the arrangement a pleasing whole and an exciting combination. Of course, the flowers should also relate to and not clash with the colour of the decor. So take into account the predominant colours of the room – the colours of the walls, carpets and furnishing fabrics – and use these as your points of reference.

Remember the colour of the container

The relationship between the colour of the container and the colours of the flowers placed in it is very important. They must work together, for the arrangement comprises both the flowers and the container, and each is as important as the other. Subdued, rustic containers like baskets will carry most combinations of flowers, whereas a brightly coloured ceramic vase, on the other hand, will be much more choosy and might overpower many flowers. However dramatic the container, the arrangement must appear inevitable.

The wonder and beauty of flowers

Do not be frightened by colour, sticking only to "safe" but boring combinations. Instead, why not experiment with using different colours? Then gradually you will come to know instinctively which colours work best together. At worst, you will create a haphazard medley of flowers or a closely matched understatement, and both of these can look beautiful in the right setting. At best, and most often, you will create an arrangement with an inexplicable but joyful touch of magic, for flowers have a way of making this happen.

The stems of African lilies continue the curve and echo the green of this beautiful iridescent, bulbous art nouveau vase, while the flowers pick up the shimmering blue.

80

—PLANT MATERIAL—
African lilies,
loosestrife and solanum

This cool froth of cow parsley bursts from the spiralled china vase. It would be ideal in an all white or pale grey room.

Similar shaped arrangements in the same container have profoundly different effects because of the use of colour. The pastel flowers (above right) create a shimmering, misty look, while the deep reds and pinks (below right) make a bolder, more emphatic statement.

—PLANT MATERIAL—
Cow parsley

**PLANT
—MATERIAL—
Freesias,
anemones, kochia
and euphorbia**

**PLANT
—MATERIAL—
Carnations,
cyclamen, spray
carnations and
camellia foliage**

Rich, strongly
contrasting colours
work together here
in a lively flower
combination that
would look good
against almost any
background. The
striking yellow of
the tansies
heightens the
pinks, reds and
lilac around it,
making them
appear stronger
and more vibrant.

—PLANT MATERIAL—
Peruvian lilies, statice,
tansies, viburnum and
melaleuca

ACCENT ON SCENT

Every bit as important as colour and form, the perfume of flowers varies from sweet and delicate to strong and spicy. Spring arrangements can be full of scent. There are the delicious hyacinths and many of the varieties of narcissus, especially jonquils and a great favourite of mine – 'Trevithian'. But when thinking of scented flowers, roses are the first that come to mind. Although I sometimes use roses with little or no scent for their unusual colours or shapes, I always try to incorporate at least a few roses with that delicious sweet, fruity "tea" scent in my summer arrangements. To me, that scent is what summer is all about. The very earliest flowering roses, such as the simple varieties like 'Canary Bird', tend to have little or no scent. Fortunately, however, the powerfully scented lily-of-the-valley also flowers at this time, which, as well as looking beautiful in a flower arrangement, more than makes up for the lack of scent in the roses.

My favourite scented roses

If you are lucky enough to live in an area where the climate is mild, you can grow *Rosa banksiae* – so profuse in Italy and the south of France – with its fragrance of rich violets. I wish that a perpetual or repeat flowering hybrid of this rose were available, for its little, creamy-yellow flowers are a delight to look at and its scent, sheer joy. Some of the best scents belong to the old roses: the heady-scented Damasks and Hybrid Musks, the clear, sweet-scented Rugosas and, from among the China roses, those with a rich tea scent. More and more roses are now being produced that have both the beautiful looks of the old-fashioned roses, with their flat, well-quartered flowers, and delicious scents. This makes a welcome change after several decades of roses produced only for their Hybrid Tea shapes, which often had little or no scent.

A plethora of fragrances

Few people are aware that at this time of year, irises have a very special perfume. The scent has a strange quality about it, often very sweet and violet-like with a slight rubbery smell on top. It sounds horrible but it isn't at all. Then there are the sweet peas. Their flower petals resemble butterflies and, like butterflies, their perfume wafts lightly and delicately on the air, one small bunch easily scenting a whole room.

With the arrival of high summer come the pinks, with their clove scents, and the lilies. Strongest-scented of all the lilies are the auratum lilies whose scent is almost overpowering: richly spicy, like concentrated nutmeg and vanilla. The perfume of the tobacco plant is similar, although not quite so heavy. Surprisingly, the tobacco plant flowers last quite well after picking and are ideal for arrangements. In autumn, the belladonna lily flowers, giving out a sugary, medicinal scent. In winter no garden is complete without some wintersweet – *Chimonanthus praecox*. On sunny days its cream-coloured, waxy bells have a scent reminiscent of gardenias.

Take every chance to use scented flowers in arrangements and in gifts of bouquets and posies. A room perfumed with flowers is wonderful, and there is nothing nicer than to receive a present of flowers that not only look beautiful but impart their delicious scent to a room.

A single hyacinth adds delicious scent to a spring arrangement.

Two sweet perfumes emanate from this simple arrangement. The scent of the hyacinths carries beautifully in the air, while that of the violets is much less pervasive. You need to draw close to the beautiful, little flowers to smell their delicate perfume.

—PLANT MATERIAL—
Hyacinths and violets

*T*here are a host of spring flowers with delicious scents that can be used in arrangements to perfume your rooms. Possibly the loveliest scent of all is that of lily-of-the-valley, which flowers late into the spring and early summer. Other spring flowers with particularly sweet perfumes are hyacinths, lilac, narcissus and mimosa.

The spicy scent of pink hyacinths combines with fragrant wattle in this informal bunch.

Buttery-scented grape hyacinths mix well with sugar-sweet polyanthus.

Only some violets have a perfume, and sadly they do not last long once cut.

Dainty wax flowers have a particularly aromatic perfume when they are cut. Here they are mixed with sweet-scented lily-of-the-valley.

Tulips have an interesting peppery scent which combines well with the heady-scented sprays of lilac.

The scents of lavender and rosemary mingle as they do in cottage gardens (right).

Of all the freesias, the coloured single flowers have the very best clear, sweet perfume (below).

Stocks and phlox make an intensely spicy scented bouquet (above).

Tuberoses combined with honeysuckle and lemon-scented geranium leaves make a heady perfume (left).

Narcissus and jasmine lend this bouquet a sweet and spicy scent.

Summer is the sweetest time of year for scent. The most fragrant summer flowers of all are the sweet peas and roses, but paeonies, irises and pinks also have lovely perfumes. Why not take the opportunity to give a friend or relative a posy or bouquet of scented flowers to fill their home with summer fragrance?

*A **simple bunch** of glorious Tea roses has a fruity scent (left).*

The opulent fragrance of lilies (below) is especially strong in the evenings. Just one bunch can scent a whole house.

There is nothing quite as lovely as a posy of sweet peas (left).

Sweet-scented sweet peas, simply arranged in a wavy glass vase, are like a cloud of pastel-coloured butterflies. Delicate and pretty flowers, their perfume is incomparable.

—PLANT MATERIAL—
Sweet peas

Aromatic thyme
Thymus vulgaris

Woodland pine
Pinus sylvestris

Tangy marigolds
Calendula officinalis

Pot pourri

Roses
Rosa cv.

Sad cypress
Cupressus sempervirens

Delicate mimosa
Acacia longifolia

Aromatic bay
Laurus nobilis

Rose flower
Rosa cv.

Exotic gardenia
Gardenia jasminoides

Clove pink
Dianthus 'Robin Thain'

Fragrant plant material such as rose petals, myrrh, iris or orris root and frankincense have been used in perfumes for centuries. The ancient Egyptians, Greeks and Romans all used these plants in fragrant mixes both for everyday use and special occasions. Derived from the French, meaning a rotten pot, pot pourri is a perfumed mixture of dried flowers and petals. "Rotten" seems to me a singularly inappropriate word to describe any of the delicious and fragrant floral combinations devised since ancient times. We may have refined the process a little, but the basic recipes for pot pourri and the methods of making the mixes remain much the same as then.

Making pot pourri

There are two methods of making pot pourri: the moist method and the dry method. For both methods the flowers should be picked just as the buds open, preferably on a dry day after any dew has evaporated. Picking the flowers then maximizes their fragrant qualities.

Using the moist method, the fragrant flower petals are first dried in part by laying them on a sheet of absorbent material such as cheesecloth or blotting paper. After a couple of days, when the petals have shrunk and are about half dry, they are placed in a jar in alternate layers with salt. This flower and salt mixture is stirred every day for about a fortnight, by which time it should be dry and crumbly. At this point, a fixative, such as orris root or tonka beans – which is essential to seal in the scent – together with spices and essential oils, are added and the jar sealed. The mixture is left for about six weeks to mature.

With the dry method, the fragrant petals and flowers are firstly dried completely. This takes about 10 days or even more, depending on the density of the flowers. Once dry, the flowers and petals are mixed with fixative, spices and oils, and placed in a jar to mature. The jar is sealed and shaken every day for about six weeks until ready for use.

Beautiful decorations, wonderful gifts

Put pot pourris in small bowls and place them on display around the house. To make them especially decorative, add some large, colourful dried-flower petals when you set them out. Pot pourris scent the air for many months before they start to fade, and even then the perfumes can be reawakened with some essential oils.

Do not stop at arranging pot pourri in bowls. Put some in linen or cotton bags and place them in drawers where the scent will perfume your clothes, or lay them between sheets and towels in the linen cupboard or between pillows. You could even simply hang them in the kitchen or bathroom. Pot pourri bags are easy to make and are ideal to give on special or festive occasions.

Sweet-perfumed rose petals
Rosa cv.

Sharp tangy santolina
Santolina chamaecyparissus

Fragrant pansies
Viola × wittrockiana

Pungent eucalyptus
Eucalyptus gunnii

Spicy stocks
Matthiola bicornis

Fresh apple mint
Mentha rotundifolia

Perfumed rose petals
Rosa cv.

Pungent tansy
Tanacetum vulgare

Delicate sweet pea
Lathyrus odorata

Lily-of-the-valley
Convallaria majalis

Rose flowers
Rosa cv.

Orange lime and lemon peel
Citrus spp.

Pot pourri recipes

Below are a few favourite recipes for some wonderfully perfumed pot pourris (illustrated overleaf).

Lavender mix

This mixture usually requires some lavender oil unless the lavender has a strong scent.

—INGREDIENTS—
2 cups lavender flowers
2 cups fragrant rose petals
1 cup rosemary leaves
2 cups lemon verbena leaves
1 cup chamomile flowers
½ cup powdered orris root
½ cup dried lemon peel
6 drops lavender oil
(optional)
Dry method
1 Dry the flowers and leaves thoroughly
2 Add the orris root and lemon peel
3 If necessary stir in the lavender oil drop by drop
4 Seal and leave to mature for six weeks

Woodland mix
—INGREDIENTS—
2 cups small fir cones
2 cups cedar twigs
2 cups sandalwood shavings
2 cups white cedar sprays
2 tablespoons orris root powder
4 drops cedarwood oil
4 drops sandalwood oil
Dry method
1 Mix together fir cones, cedar twigs, sandalwood shavings, cedar sprays and orris root powder
2 Stir in oils drop by drop
3 Store in a sealed container for six weeks

Simple rose mix

A deliciously fragrant pot pourri. The rose perfume can be intensified by the addition of a few drops of rose oil.

—INGREDIENTS—
10 cups very fragrant rose petals
1 cup rose geranium leaves
1 cup coarse salt
½ cup powdered orris root
1 tablespoon ground cloves
1 tablespoon ground allspice
5 drops lemon oil
Moist method
1 Part dry rose petals and rose geranium leaves for two days
2 Layer with salt
3 Stir mixture daily for a fortnight
4 Add remaining ingredients
5 Seal and leave to cure for six weeks

Spicy mix
—INGREDIENTS—
10 cups fragrant flower petals, such as roses, pinks, irises, paeonies and marigolds
2 cups coarse salt
2 cups crushed coriander sticks
½ cup thinly sliced ginger
2 tablespoons ground nutmeg
Moist method
1 Part dry flower petals for two days
2 Layer in 1.5cm (½in) bands with salt
3 Stir mixture daily for a fortnight
4 Add remaining ingredients
5 Seal and store for six weeks

Seedy mix
—INGREDIENTS—
1 cup aniseed
1 cup coriander seeds
1 cup rose hips
½ cup cardamom seeds
½ cup juniper berries
1 cup cedar cone seeds
½ cup allspice
½ cup dried orange peel
½ cup dried lime peel
6 ground tonka beans
6 drops patchouli oil
Dry method
1 Mix the seeds, spice, peel and ground beans together
2 Stir in the patchouli oil drop by drop
3 Seal and store for six weeks

Spring mix

A delicate mixture.
—INGREDIENTS—
2 cups fragrant narcissus flowers
1 cup lily of the valley flowers
2 cups mimosa flowers
1 cup lilac flowers
1 cup parma violets
1 cup wallflowers
2 cups coarse salt
½ cup orris root powder
3 drops lily-of-the-valley oil
Moist method
1 Part dry the flowers for two days
2 Layer the flowers in 1.5cm (½in) bands with the salt
3 Stir mixture daily for a fortnight
4 Add orris root
5 Stir in lily-of-the-valley oil drop by drop
6 Seal and set aside for six weeks to mature

Seedy mix

Lavender mix

*F*rom the host of pot pourri recipes to choose from (see p.95), here are just a few mixes, ranging widely in scent and ingredients. As their perfumes fade, rejuvenate them with some essential oils or even a little brandy.

Seedy mix A rich, oriental, spicy scent emanates from this pot pourri, which contains star anise, cardamoms and coriander mixed with citrus and patchouli oil.

Lavender mix The strong, old-fashioned perfume of lavender flowers is heightened by the rosemary, verbena and chamomile.

Spring mix This pot pourri has a wonderfully light scent. The mimosa perfume carries well but the most pervasive scent comes from the lily-of-the-valley.

Woodland mix Forest scents emanate from this attractive-looking pot pourri. Combining orris with both cedar and sandalwood makes a really interesting perfume.

Summer mix Marigolds, roses, paeonies, pinks and irises are just a few of the fragrant flowers that comprise this pot pourri. Its rich, summery perfume is laced with cinnamon and cloves.

Rose mix The scent of this pot pourri epitomizes summer. The lemon and rose geranium leaves add richness to the overall perfume.

Summer mix

Rose mix

Woodland mix

Spring mix (far left)

FLOWERS & FOOD

To make good food all the more delicious, simply add flowers, not only as decoration for the table, breakfast tray, or picnic rug, but also to garnish any sort of dish, from salads and sandwiches to fish and fruit, and from cakes and confections to meat and vegetables. A single rose or a few flowers arranged in a vase can make a simple meal seem a little bit special. Likewise, the ritual Sunday morning breakfast in bed with the papers is brightened no end by the addition of a few flowers on the breakfast tray, even if you have to put them there yourself! Of course, it is even better when the flowers – and the breakfast – arrive as a waking surprise.

A simple bunch of flowers set beside you in the kitchen when you are cooking never fails to inspire. Make sure that they are out of harm's way, but clearly visible – perhaps on the window sill or on the corner of a work surface. Then, if the meal is progressing well, they are there to share your delight and if things start to go wrong – perhaps a pot boils over – their presence will make the mishap seem so much less disastrous.

A few single flowers make this tiered stand of fancy biscuits, sweetmeats and crystallized fruit all the more decorative on the dinner table.

Entertaining with flowers

Whether you are planning a lunch for friends, a Sunday roast for eight, a romantic dinner for two, or a grand dinner party, make sure you include an arrangement or two to help create a relaxed atmosphere.

Arrangements for such occasions need not be elaborate. In fact, a simple flower would make the perfect table centrepiece at the dinner for two. If you are entertaining several people and wish to create a larger arrangement, make sure that it is not so wide or tall as to make conversation difficult with the person seated opposite. Reflect some of the colours of the room, tablecloth or napkins, even the colours of the food, in the flowers you choose, and try using some fruit or vegetables in the arrangement. Cherries, blackberries, strawberries, curly kale, cabbage leaves and sprigs of herbs can all look absolutely beautiful amongst flowers.

For a candle-lit dinner under the shimmering night sky, try scented white flowers. A summer picnic demands a crock of brilliant flowers that sing their colours against meadow-green or water-blue. The vivid reds and yellows of tropical flowers would suit perfectly an exotic dinner in a conservatory.

Put flowers on the menu!

Many flowers, decorative fruits and vegetables are good to eat, and it is undoubtedly true that the more beautiful a dish looks, the more delicious it tastes. There are plenty of edible flowers that can be added to salads. The startling red, orange and yellow flowers of tasty nasturtiums make a strong visual impact when set against the bright greens of lettuce or dark greens of spinach, pale chicory or frilly endive. Sweet-scented rose petals, marigolds, violets, primroses, fruit tree blossoms and the flowers of many herbs all make beautiful garnishes to a dish. Violets, rose petals, primroses, cherry blossom, freesias and mint leaves can all be crystallized, using either a mixture of egg white and sugar or gum arabic and sugar. These sweet-flavoured flowers and leaves make delectable decorations for all manner of puddings, gâteaux and cakes, and provide a very distinctive finishing touch.

The brilliant blue of these gentians is accentuated by the delicate china on this breakfast tray. The glass sugar bowl makes an ideal container.

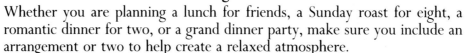

—PLANT MATERIAL—
Gentians

A delicious mix of cool colours, this salad (left) has a base of chicory with the flowers of fennel and young chives added as decoration. A lime dressing is ideal for this combination.

No salad is complete without the addition of some garden flowers. While some are both attractive in colour and shape and delicious, many others are not good to eat and are best used only for decoration. Most of the flowers of herbs have a simple wild look and the same taste as the leaves, making them ideal for salads or savoury dishes.

Curly-edged, pinky-rust endive has a slightly bitter taste but it blends well with the flavour of little sprigs of aromatic thyme flowers, sweet and delicate-flavoured pink, scented rose petals and tiny white flowers of chamomile (right). Together they make a delicious mix that is especially tasty with a mustard dressing.

This colourful combination
of reds, oranges and yellows
(above) is set off by the pale
green lettuce base and glowing
nasturtium flowers (which
have a tangy taste like
watercress), marigold and
dandelion flowers, and a few
pink runner bean flowers. A
walnut oil dressing is the ideal
accompaniment.

Crystallized flowers

Crystallized flowers are easy to prepare and, as well as looking beautiful, they are delicious to eat. Almost any flowers can be crystallized, the best ones being violets, primroses, scented rose petals, fruit blossom and small edible leaves such as mint and lemon balm, but it is important to make sure that you do not use any that are poisonous.

There are two methods of crystallizing flowers. The simplest uses egg white and sugar, while the second, using gum arabic and sugar, lasts longer.

Egg white method
Beat an egg white until it is just mixed and has lost its glutinous consistency. With a small paintbrush, paint the egg white evenly all over the petal surfaces of the flowers. Sprinkle the flowers immediately with caster sugar, and leave to dry in a warm place.

Gum arabic method
Put 12g (½oz) gum arabic in a basin with a quarter cupful of cold water. Place the basin in a pan of water or a double boiler set over medium heat, and stir the mixture until it has dissolved. Allow it to cool, then brush the mixture on the flower petals and sprinkle with caster sugar. Leave the flowers to dry in a warm place for a couple of hours.

Two iced sponge cakes are decorated with crystallized flowers, one with primroses, pear and cherry blossom and tiny narcissus, and the other with sweet-scented violets, borage and auriculas. All but the narcissus flowers are edible and delicious, but the violet leaves are simply for decoration.

—PLANT MATERIAL—
Grapes, vine and fig leaves, mulberries, blackberries, nectarines, pineapple, runner beans, ornamental cabbage leaves, crab apples, pears and dahlias

To make this sumptuous arrangement, fix a lipped tray and three plastic bowls to a lazy-Susan dish with adhesive clay. Then fix plastic prongs to the base of each, and place mounds of wet foam on top. Build up the arrangement gradually from one side of the dish to the other. Insert the unwired stems firmly into the foam and set the fruit directly upon the dish. Sit the pineapple on the raised centre plate to provide the glorious finishing touch.

This grand mixture of seasonal fruits, vegetables and flowers would make a sumptuous arrangement for a dinner party. Designed as a facing arrangement, it would be ideal for a sideboard.

FLOWERS & PLANTS

Arrangements that combine plants and cut flowers and foliage are always interesting to create. Such an arrangement must be large enough to encompass the plant in its pot and the cut flowers. The growing plant, once placed in the arrangement, usually lasts extremely well. Low containers that are a little taller than the height of the pot are ideal for these combination arrangements. Baskets, ceramic bowls, copper and brass dishes, even wooden fruit boxes all make excellent receptacles for plant and flower arrangements. The garden can be an inspiration in this matter: a wooden earth sieve or trug can be annexed for a combination arrangement. Any porous container must be lined first with plastic and the pots should be wedged into position with wet foam. You can then use the foam for holding the flowers and foliage.

Flower and plant arrangements can look elegant given a sophisticated vase such as this two-tiered one.

Simple plant and flower arrangements

The simplest arrangement of this sort is one using a single type of plant or perhaps just one plant in a cache pot with a few cut flowers surrounding it. Make sure the container complements the plant that is used. Simple plants like primroses or African violets look particularly well arranged in a mossy basket with cut flowers at the sides. Small grape hyacinths, snowdrops and narcissi look good with primroses and freesias, while miniature roses and brodiaea can look stunning with African violets.

The problem of watering

Watering the plants can be a problem if the pots have no drainage hole; it is important that plants do not sit in soggy soil as this can cause root rot. It is often best to keep the plants in the pots that they have grown in, rather than planting them into the container. Then they can be removed carefully for watering one by one. If the arrangement is to stand outside, then it is better to plant directly into a container with a drainage hole. Most pot plants love to be outside in a semi-shady spot throughout the summer; an outdoor arrangement can also make an attractive feature, especially if it is sited on a table or the ground just outside the house where it can be seen from inside.

The delightful Primula scotica.

Cool indoor locations are ideal

Inside or in the conservatory you have a wide choice of pot plants. There are always begonias in a wide range of colours, especially the apricots, pinks, reds and creams. There are also succulent kalanchoes, which produce flowers in bright red, shocking pink and yellow over a very long period. Azaleas, which are available throughout the winter and spring, are very colourful and must be kept well watered to give of their best. Any of these plants can be combined with cut flowers for a special occasion, and it is always worth keeping an eye open for an unusual container.

At Christmas time the shops are full of poinsettias in brilliant red, pink, cream and white. These can look wonderful used in a mixed festive arrangement with cut berried holly and winter foliage, such as pine or cedar. The flowers of orchid plants last for many weeks. These can look exciting in a mixed arrangement with other exotic flowers of sympathetic colourings or simply with foliage and other green plants.

The pretty woodland primrose, Primula vulgaris.

This old-fashioned primrose basket is first lined with perforated plastic and bun moss before planting the primroses inside.

PLANT —MATERIAL— Primroses and bun moss

**PLANT
—MATERIAL—
Orchids, anemones,
mind-your-own-
business and
dryandra**

*To make this
arrangement,* line a
vine twig basket with
plastic. Place two
orchid plants at the
back and two plastic
bowls of wet foam at
the front. Arrange the
anemones and the
dryandra leaves in the
foam, and surround
the orchid plants with
mind-your-own-
business.

*T*he interesting
mixture of textures
and colours in this
arrangement give it a
special character. The
rough bark of the vine
twigs cradles the low
mound of plant
material and flowers,
while the two orchid
blooms and their spiky
leaves loom overhead.
The orchids dominate
the display because of
their prominent
position, but the other
surrounding plants,
foliage and flowers
add interesting
textures and colour.

*F*ive cineraria plants nestle between three wet-foam-filled bowls containing groups of white ranunculus, cornflowers and their foliage, and the delicate stems of brodiaea in this decorative, multi-coloured wicker basket.

—PLANT MATERIAL—
Cineraria, cornflowers, ranunculus and brodiaea

Flowers in their seasons

During the course of the year we are provided with an enormous wealth of plant material, which alters from week to week throughout the seasons. At the end of winter, there is that magic moment when the first crocuses and daffodils appear from an earth that had looked as though it would never support plant life again. Suddenly the fields and hedgerows come alive with flowers and foliage, the colour yellow predominating. In summer the colour range is reversed, with plenty of pink, red and blue flowers and occasional patches of yellow just for good measure.

Autumn throws up more mellow colours: rusts, reds, ambers, golds and oranges dominate the borders, although there are still some pale pinks, creams and white around. In winter there are fewer flowers and we have to rely more on the dark greens of evergreen foliage and the reds of winter berries.

SPRING

An exciting freshness fills the air in spring – the season of rejuvenation. It is as though a great weight has been lifted from our spirits. Colour begins to come into its own again, and the sky seems that much clearer. There may be showers, but the clouds are soon broken by patches of bright blue sky. The evenings are lighter and there is a softness in the breeze. Suddenly the growing process, which slowed down to a virtual halt during the winter months, increases almost alarmingly. One day the ground looks bare and the next it is covered with shoots several inches high. The process is undoubtedly slightly slower but it certainly doesn't seem that way.

Of all the seasons, spring, particularly, is a time for bulbs. The very earliest bulbs – the winter aconites, snowdrops and crocuses – finish with the end of winter, leaving the way clear for that wonderful family of bulbs, the narcissus. Commonest of all is the daffodil with its bold trumpet of bright yellow surrounded by a halo of petals. Daffodils are tough specimens and can easily withstand the strong spring winds without being damaged. They are great favourites as cut flowers, and last well, especially if they are placed in a cool position. There are dozens of varieties of narcissus. Some are like the common daffodil in shape, but have different coloured petals and perianths (the trumpet in the centre), while some are much smaller. There are also a host of double and multi-flowered varieties, most of which have a strong, sweet perfume such as 'Cheerfulness' and 'Bridal Crown'. My favourites of the varieties with several flowers to the stem are the jonquils. Their flowers are like little daffodils and their scent is absolutely delicious.

Abundance of spring bulbs

At the same time that the daffodils are out, so too are hyacinths in pinks, blues, whites and creams, and the sky-blue scillas and chionodoxa. A little later, the tulips start to bloom. They have an enormous colour range: from almost black through pinks and reds and oranges to yellows, creams, white and green. Many are also splashed with two or more colours, especially the parrot tulips. They make lovely cut flowers, twisting and curving into interesting shapes as they grow in the vase.

Lilies-of-the-valley, which produce delicate spires of flowers with an incomparable perfume, also bloom at this time of year. Fritillaries, too, flower in the spring. There are the delicate snake's head bells of *Fritillaria meleagris* and the great hanging circle of trumpets of the crown imperials, *Fritillaria imperialis*, which make good cut flowers for displaying in spring arrangements if you don't mind their rather rancid smell.

Other lovely flowers are the wallflowers, which look attractive growing amongst tulips and with a perfume that reminds us of the coming summer months. Rhododendrons and azaleas, too, display their blaze of colour towards the end of spring. They are the virtuosi of shrubs with blooms of blinding pinks and oranges, pure whites and yellows, and rich reds. The smaller varieties last quite well if they are cut just as the buds begin to open.

As spring gets under way, however, the days become warmer and the hours of sunlight longer, and all too soon the bulbs are over and beginning to save up their energies for next year's appearance.

Camellias
Camellia 'Leonard Messel'

Pansies
Viola wittrockiana 'Roggli Giant'

Snake's head fritillaries
Fritillaria meleagris

Oxlips
Primula elatior

Plants in **bold** type are
shown on pp.116–121.
Acacia dealbata
Acacia longifolia
Acacia pravissima
Aesculus hippocastanum
Ajuga reptans
Anemone coronaria
Anthriscus sylvestris
Anthurium
Arum italicum
Bergenia cordifolia
Bergenia stracheyi
Brassica
Buxus sempervirens
Camellia japonica
Chaenomeles japonica
Chaenomeles speciosa
Cheiranthus cheiri
Chionodoxa luciliae
Choisya ternata
Cineraria cruenta
Clivia miniata
Convallaria majalis
Cornus florida
Cornus mas
Cornus nuttallii
Corylopsis pauciflora
Corylus avellana
Crataegus monogyna
Crocus
Cyclamen repandum
Cymbidium
Cytisus × praecox
Cytisus scoparius
Daphne mezereum

Dicentra spectabilis
Doronicum pardalianches
Doronicum plantagineum
Dryandra
Erica arborea
Erica carnea
Erythronium dens-canis
Euphorbia characias
Euphorbia rigida
Forsythia × intermedia
Fothergilla monticola
Fritillaria imperialis
Fritillaria meleagris
Gentiana verna
Halesia carolina
Helleborus
Hippeastrum
Hyacinthoides hispanica
Hyacinthoides non-scripta

Narcissi
Narcissus 'Liberty Bells'

Hyacinthus orientalis
Iberis
Iris
Ixia
Lachenalia aloides
Larix leptolepis
Magnolia
Mahonia bealei
Mahonia japonica
Malus
Muscari armeniacum
Myosotis alpestris
Myosotis sylvatica
Narcissus
Ornithogalum umbellatum
Pieris
Polemonium
Polygonatum commutatum
Polygonatum × hybridum

Grape hyacinths
Muscari armeniacum

Primula malacoides
Primula obconica
Primula vulgaris
Prunus
Pulmonaria officinalis
Pulmonaria saccharata
Pulsatilla vulgaris
Pyrus
Ranunculus asiaticus
Rheum rhaponticum
Rhododendron
Ribes sanguineum
Rosmarinus lavandulaceus
Rosmarinus officinalis
Salix apoda
Salix incana
Sambucus
Scilla bifolia
Scilla sibirica
Skimmia japonica
Sorbus
Spiraea
Strelitzia reginae
Syringa
Trollius
Tulipa
Ulex europaeus
Viburnum burkwoodii
Viburnum × carlcephalum
Viburnum carlesii
Viburnum × juddii
Viburnum opulus
Vinca major
Vinca minor
Viola odorata
Zantedeschia aethiopica

Sweet violet
Viola odorata

The tiny flowers that nestle beneath the leaves are very sweetly scented.

Forsythia
Forsythia × intermedia

White dead nettle
Lamium album

Rosemary
Rosmarinus officinalis

Orchid
Cymbidium hybrid

Borage
Borago officinalis

These intensely blue star flowers are attractive in drinks or salads.

Forget-me-not
Myosotis alpestris

This wonderful blue spring flower self-seeds to produce new plants each year.

Spiraea
Spiraea thunbergii

Wreathed in tiny, delicate white flowers in spring, spiraea lasts well in water.

Jew's mallow
Kerria japonica 'Pleniflora'

Guelder rose
Viburnum opulus
'Roseum'

Primrose
Primula vulgaris

Primula
Primula denticulata

Hyacinth
Hyacinthus orientalis

Daffodil
Narcissus 'Sir Winston
Churchill'

Daffodil
Narcissus 'Professor
Einstein'

Daffodil
Narcissus 'Kingscourt'

Periwinkle
Vinca major

Daffodil
Narcissus 'Interim'

Daffodil
Narcissus 'Golden Lion'

Daffodil
Narcissus 'Tahiti'

Wild daffodil
*Narcissus
pseudonarcissus*

Spring snowflake
Leucojum vernum

This large version of
the snowflake will easily
naturalize in the garden.

Daffodil
Narcissus
'Silver Chimes'

Grape hyacinth
Muscari armeniacum

Polyanthus
Primula Polyanthus

Cowslip
Primula veris

Comfrey
Symphytum orientale
The drooping trumpet
flowers are borne in
profusion over a long
period in late spring.

Skimmia
Skimmia japonica

Decorative crab
Malus floribunda
A beautifully shaped tree with deep pink flowerbuds opening almost white.

Anemone
Anemone coronaria 'The Bride'

Decorative crab
Malus × lemoinei

Pear
Pyrus communis

Tulip *Tulipa praecox*

Tulip
Tulipa 'Golden Mirjoran'

Auricula
Primula Auricula
Sweet scented and in an amazing range of greens, greys, plums and yellows, these flowers have been hybridized for centuries.

Bethlehem sage
Pulmonaria saccharata
Both the spotted leaves and the pink flowers that turn blue as they fade are very decorative.

Tulip
Tulipa 'Angélique'

Azalea
Rhododendron cv.

Decorative cherry
Prunus sargentii

Snake's head fritillary
Fritillaria meleagris

Flowering currant
Ribes sanguineum

Flowering quince
Chaenomeles speciosa

Wallflower
Cheiranthus cheiri

Although available all-year-round from flower shops, these beautiful white anemones are at their best in spring.

Lilac
Syringa vulgaris 'Mme Florent Stepman'

Camellia
Camellia japonica

Tulip
Tulipa 'Estella Rijnveld'

Pansy
Viola × wittrockiana

Lenten rose
Helleborus orientalis

Viburnum
Viburnum carlesii 'Aurora'

Wild pansy
Viola tricolor

Magnolia
Magnolia kobus

These magnolia flowers are exquisite. The buds will open in water.

Pasqueflower
Pulsatilla vulgaris
The nodding heads of these beautiful flowers have downy outsides to their petals.

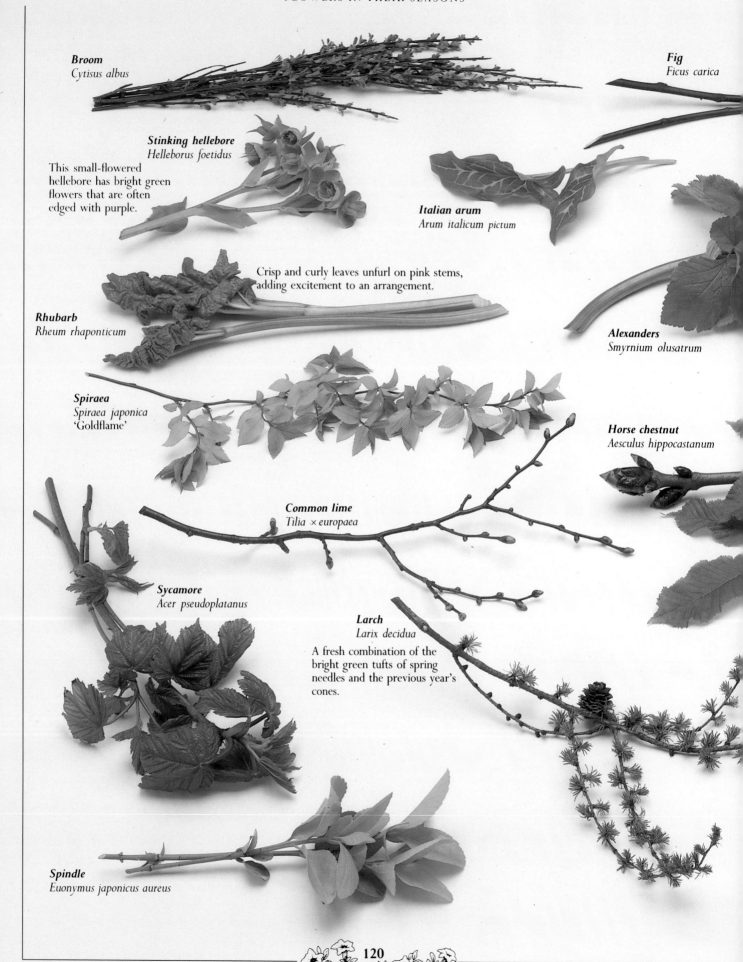

Broom
Cytisus albus

Fig
Ficus carica

Stinking hellebore
Helleborus foetidus

This small-flowered hellebore has bright green flowers that are often edged with purple.

Italian arum
Arum italicum pictum

Crisp and curly leaves unfurl on pink stems, adding excitement to an arrangement.

Rhubarb
Rheum rhaponticum

Alexanders
Smyrnium olusatrum

Spiraea
Spiraea japonica
'Goldflame'

Horse chestnut
Aesculus hippocastanum

Common lime
Tilia × europaea

Sycamore
Acer pseudoplatanus

Larch
Larix decidua

A fresh combination of the bright green tufts of spring needles and the previous year's cones.

Spindle
Euonymus japonicus aureus

Honeysuckle
Lonicera periclymenum
'Belgica'

Hornbeam
Carpinus betulus

The trails of catkins open
in mid-spring and are
followed by winged seeds.

Pussy willow
Salix caprea

The stems of pussy
willow last for
several weeks in an
arrangement,
although it is
advisable to change
the water frequently
to prevent it from
smelling.

Lilac
Syringa vulgaris

It is best to remove
all the leaves from
lilac stems before
arranging them, to
enable the flowers to
flourish to full
capacity.

Mrs Robb's bonnet
*Euphorbia amygdaloides
robbiae*

The golden green flowers rise well above
the rich, dark evergreen leaves.

121

—— *Arranging spring flowers* ——

*I*f you have a garden, spring is the time to start picking flowers for arrangements in the house. Almost overnight daffodils, hyacinths and cherry blossom are beckoning brightly, followed soon after by tulips. With their bright joyful colours, and their simple, appealing shapes, spring flowers seem to demand more informal treatment than flowers from other seasons. Often a simple bunch of spring flowers in a glass jar can have just as much appeal as a very formal arrangement.

Most of the narcissus family have fleshy stems so they need containers with necks that will hold their stems in place. A simple jam jar or cylindrical glass container is ideal for this purpose. As daffodil stems are so regimented, they look really good through clear glass. Tulip stems, on the other hand, tend to make interesting shapes once they are arranged and they can, in fact, go on growing in the vase for several days.

Stems of cherry blossom and lilac like to be given a quick boil before arranging and then will last surprisingly well. Removing lilac leaves will also help to make the blossom last. Another beautiful, late spring flower is ranunculus. Its stems can sometimes be quite soft, however, and will need to be supported amongst other flowers, or you can push stub wires up the stems before arranging them.

All these spring flowers will last well provided it is cool, so don't place them too close to a radiator.

*T*hese very unusual Cape cowslips, with their lime green open bells and bright orange buds look best displayed on their own in a simple, glazed earthenware pot.

—**PLANT MATERIAL**—
Cape cowslips

A glass jam jar can look just as beautiful as an expensive vase when filled with spring flowers, although it would really be more suitable for an informal setting such as a kitchen window ledge. All these spring flowers last better if they are kept cool, even outside on a table.

—PLANT MATERIAL—
Double and single daffodils, hyacinths, forsythia, widow iris, lily-of-the-valley and alder catkins

*T*his cheerful and sunny
mixed spring arrangement is
simply and informally
displayed in an old blue and
cream Spanish bowl. The
colours of the bowl link in well
with the cream of the heath
and the blues of the grape
hyacinths and forget-me-nots.
The whole arrangement is
strengthened by the pussy
willow twigs while the splash
of pink at the side seems to
enhance the cooler colours.

—PLANT MATERIAL—
**Pussy willow, heath, grape
hyacinths, forget-me-nots,
narcissi and rhododendrons**

A clear glass vase makes a beautiful container for these joyful and informal spring flowers. The pink of the ranunculus blooms works beautifully with the pure white lilac and cherry blossom. The arrangement gives an impression of movement, as if the flowers are springing out of the vase.

—PLANT MATERIAL—
Lilac, cherry blossom and ranunculus

A rich golden shower of fluffy mimosa flowers spills from this blue glass vase, highlighting its gold and deeper blue decorations. The arrangement epitomizes the way that mimosa grows naturally, its great branches weighed down with their sweetly scented flowers.

—PLANT MATERIAL—
Mimosa

*An interesting,
bulbous strawberry pot
here contains a spring
planting of crocuses
and a single hyacinth.*

*T*his low mossy mound covered with spring flowers and trails of ivy would make an unusual and ravishing centrepiece for a large dining table and is very easy to make. The base is a large plate covered first with a thin layer of wet foam and then with moss. Stems of spring flowers and ivy are then pushed through the moss into the foam. The arrangement will last well if the foam is kept wet.

—**PLANT MATERIAL**—
Narcissi, tulips, ranunculus, ivy and moss

SUMMER

Long, sunny days are what summer is all about. And the most wonderful time of the day in summer is the early morning. It is a time to sit in the garden and have a quiet breakfast surrounded by the humming haze of soft light with its promise of the sunny day to come. Summer is the most comfortable time of the year: there is no need for cumbersome and heavy clothes, and the daylight hours are long so that we can make the most of being outdoors. This also suits the plants, which respond by putting on a lovely display, each outdoing the next with its colour and form. The tulips, rhododendrons and azaleas of spring now give way to irises, paeonies and roses, and all of these seem to spell out summer in a most sumptuous way.

Irises, with their subtle colourings and interesting perfume, have beautifully formed flowers that grow upwards from their silvery, angular leaves. Paeonies – both the single- and double-flowered varieties – are beautiful and voluptuous flowers, but it is the double ones that make the best cut flowers. Pick or buy them as the buds start to open and they should last for nearly a week before the great balls of petals begin to fall apart. They have a sweet buttery smell, too. I would find it difficult to state a colour preference: red, white and pink paeonies are all equally beautiful in arrangements.

Favourite summer flowers

At the same time as the paeonies are blooming, the roses begin their long flowering season. Although these shrubs do not have the most attractive growing habit, their flowers are the best loved in the world. They have been grown since early times and their perfume was extracted by the ancient Greeks and Romans. The Victorians and Edwardians produced an enormous number of new rose hybrids, some like *Rosa* 'Paul Neyron' with flowers as large as and resembling a double paeony. In the 1950s, 60s and 70s the accent was on producing Hybrid Teas, and sadly many of these had little or no scent. Now there is a movement to produce roses that combine the good attributes of the old-fashioned roses in their form of flower and rich scent, together with a perpetual flowering habit, which many of the old roses did not have. Roses are not very long lasting once they have been cut, but this is more than compensated for by the fact that they look so beautiful in a vase, when you can look at their flowers in detail and appreciate their perfume. Double-flowered blooms last much longer than the single ones.

Another wonderful flower for cutting is mock orange, which flowers in the early summer. This has one of the best scents of all. Flowering branches for arranging are best if they have their leaves removed, as the flowers will then last longer. My favourite variety is *Philadelphus* 'Belle Etoile' with its large flowers blotched purple at the base and its lovely rich scent. Next come the lilies, phlox, the towering delphiniums, and the colourful poppies, geraniums and lavender, all of which can be used in arrangements. At the same time, there are many annuals that are excellent for picking and last well in water, such as larkspur, snapdragons, stocks and godetias.

Summer always seems to be the longest of all the seasons, which is lovely as it is so colourful. With the abundance of flowers blooming during these months, it is the best time for arranging flowers – so make the most of it!

Shirley poppies
Papaver rhoeas

Paeonies
Paeonia 'Silver Flare'

Irises
Iris laevigata

Roses
Rosa 'Mrs John Laing'

Plants in **bold** type are shown on pp.132–143.

Acanthus
Achillea
Aechmea fasciata
Agapanthus praecox
Alcea rosea
Alchemilla mollis
Allium
Alstroemeria
Anchusa azurea
Angelica archangelica
Anthemis cupaniana
Anthurium andreanum
Antirrhinum majus
Aquilegia vulgaris
Armeria
Artemisia
Asparagus officinalis
Asparagus plumosus
Astilbe × arendsii
Astrantia
Begonia
Borago officinalis
Bouvardia × domestica
Brodiaea laxa
Buddleia
Caladium × hortulanum
Calceolaria × herbeohybrida
Calendula officinalis
Callistephus chinensis
Campanula
Ceanothus
Celosia argentea
Centaurea
Centranthus ruber

Choisya ternata
Chrysanthemum
Clarkia
Clematis
Coleus blumei
Coreopsis
Cotinus coggygria
   'Foliis Purpureis'
Delphinium
Deutzia × hybrida
Dianthus
Dicentra spectabilis
Digitalis purpurea
Dimorphotheca aurantiaca
Echinops ritro
Eremurus robustus
Erica cinerea
Erigeron speciosus
Eryngium
Escallonia
Eupatorium cannabinum
Euphorbia
Freesia × kewensis
Gaillardia aristata
Gardenia jasminoides
Gentiana asclepiadea
Geranium
Gerbera jamesonii
Geum chiloense
Glaucium flavum
Gloriosa superba
Gypsophila
Hebe
Helichrysum
Heliotropium × hybridum
Helipterum manglesii

Hemerocallis citrina
Heracleum mantegazzianum
Hibiscus syriacus
Hosta
Hypericum
Iberis sempervirens
Iris
Ixia
Jasminum officinale
Laburnum
Lagurus ovatus
Lamium
Lathyrus latifolius
Lathyrus odoratus
Lavandula angustifolia
Liatris callilepis
Liatris spicata
Lilium
Lonicera americana
Lonicera japonica
Lonicera periclymenum
Luma apiculata
Lunaria annua
Lupinus
Lysimachia clethroides
Magnolia grandiflora
Magnolia sieboldii
Malva alcea
Matthiola incana
Mentha
Miltonia
Molucella laevis
Monarda didyma
Myrtus communis
Nepeta
Nicotiana

Nigella damascena
Nymphaea
Olearia
Ornithogalum thyrsoides
Paeonia
Papaver
Pelargonium
Penstemon hartwegii
Phalaris arundinacea
Philadelphus
Phlox paniculata
Phygelius
Polemonium
Polianthes tuberosa
Polygonum affine
Polygonum bistorta
Rosa
Saintpaulia ionantha
Salvia
Saponaria officinalis
Scabiosa
Senecio
Solanum
Sorbus
Spathiphyllum wallisii
Spiraea 'Arguta'
Spiraea japonica
Stachys
Thalictrum
Thymus
Tilia
Tropaeolum majus
Verbascum
Viola × wittrockiana
Wiegela florida
Zinnia elegans

Ceanothus
Ceanothus impressus

Columbine
Aquilegia

Chives
Allium schoenoprasum

Candytuft
Iberis
These lovely whorls
of white flowers
(right) are ideal for
a mixed posy.

Laburnum
Laburnum
× *watereri* 'Vossii'
The stems of this
plant, carrying
sweet-scented
racemes of flowers,
should be placed in
boiling water before
arranging (see p.42).

Ranunculus
Ranunculus asiaticus

Clematis
Clematis 'Nellie
Moser'
This beautiful, striped
clematis (right) lasts
well in an
arrangement.

Bleeding heart
Dicentra spectabilis

Snakeweed
Polygonum bistorta

Often two crops of
flowers are produced
by this plant
(above), which lasts
well when cut.

Alkanet
*Pentaglottis
sempervirens*
Stems of this blue-
flowering plant
(below) must be
boiled.

Thrift
Armeria plantaginea

Wood spurge
*Euphorbia
amygdaloides*
The stem ends of wood
spurge (right) are best
singed (see p.41) before
arranging them, to
seal them.

Spanish bluebell
Hyacinthoides campanulatus

These simple flowers
can look pretty in a
wild mix.

Broom
Cytisus × praecox

Whitebeam
Sorbus aria
'Lutescens'

Jacob's ladder
Polemonium foliosissimum

Both the blue and
white varieties of
this plant (above)
flower over a long
period.

Cow parsley
Anthriscus sylvestris

The stems of cow
parsley (above) must
be boiled before
using the plant.

One of the most beautiful
of sweet-scented flowers (below),
the flowers must be removed as they
die, so that new buds will flower.

Iris
Iris cv.

Iris
Iris ruthenica

Lily-of-the-valley
Convallaria majalis
Although not long
lasting, the scent
and delicacy of this
plant are wonderful.

Stock
Matthiola incana
The spicy scent of
stock is
intoxicating.

Sneezewort
Achillea ptarmica
A delicate
cottage garden
plant (below).

Pinks
Dianthus plumarius
hybrids

Fernleaf yarrow
Achillea 'Salmon
Beauty' and
A. 'Moonshine'
This flower (right)
lasts a long while
after cutting.

Protea
Protea 'Blushing
Bride'

This most delicate
of the sub-tropical
proteas (left) lasts well
when cut. It can also be
dried afterwards.

Spikes of catmint
flowers (loved by
cats) are produced
throughout the
summer.

Catmint
*Nepeta
gigantea*

Valerian
Centranthus ruber

Bellflower
Campanula trachelium
'Alba Plena'
This double
form (left) is
particularly
beautiful.

Allium
Allium oreophilum

Lupin
Lupinus Russell
strain
Developed from
the tree lupin,
Lupinus arboreus
and *Lupinus
polyphyllus*.

Lily
Lilium regale

Delphinium
Delphinium
Pacific hybrid

Rose
Rosa 'Golden
Wings'

Cherry
Prunus avium 'Early
Rivers'

This large, single
rose of perfect
shape has long,
pale-lemon petals
and a yellow boss
of stamens at its
centre. It has a
delicate scent, but
it does not last
long after cutting.

Protea
Protea obtusifolia
The large and
showy flowers of
most proteas
should be used
boldly.

Cornflower
Centaurea cyanus

Asparagus
Asparagus officinalis

Sweet william
Dianthus barbatus

Sweet william
Dianthus barbatus

135

Sweet pea
Lathyrus odoratus
These beautiful
cottage plants
(left) are
unfortunately
short-lived, once
cut.

Snapdragon
Antirrhinum majus

Pink rose
Rosa cv.

Yellow rose
Rosa 'Courvoisier'

Sweet pea
Lathyrus odoratus
Although the
flowers do not last
long, they have a
delicious scent.

Lilac rose
Rosa 'Variegata di
Bologna'

White everlasting pea
Lathyrus latifolius albus

Masterwort
Astrantia major
The true flowers
lie at the centre
of the bracts.

**Marguerite
or Paris daisy**
*Argyranthemum
frutescens*
All the varieties of
chrysanthemum
last well when
cut.

**Yellow horned-
poppy**
Glaucium flavum
The coarse silver-
tinged foliage of this
plant sets
off the yellow
flowers.

Shasta daisy
Leucanthemum maximum

Allium
Allium aflatunense
Onion heads are
highly decorative.

Damask rose
Rosa damascena
The sweet-scented
petals of the damask
are ideal for pot pourri.

Rose
Rosa 'Charles de
Mills'

Mock orange
Philadelphus
'Burfordensis'
The arching
branches become
weighed down
with blossom.
Their stems
should be
hammered (see
p.40) before using
in arrangements.

Pink paeony
Paeonia lactiflora cv.

White paeony
Paeonia lactiflora
'Festiva Maxima'

Tree paeony
Paeonia suffruticosa

Astilbe
Astilbe × *arendsii*

Love-in-a-mist
Nigella damascena

Brodiaea
Brodiaea laxa

The many
flowered umbels
of these flowers
resemble miniature
African lilies.

Foxglove
Digitalis purpurea

The tall spires of
this woodland
plant (below) make
excellent cut
flowers.

Butterfly bush
Buddleia davidii

A favourite of
butterflies, the
stems of these
scented plumes
must be boiled
before arranging
(see p.42). Even so
there is always a
number of dead
flowers and buds
on each flower
cluster.

Giant hogweed
*Heracleum
mantegazzianum*

Globe thistle
Echinops ritro

Chincherinchee
*Ornithogalum
thyrsoides*

Swamp lily
Lilium superbum

Veronica
Veronica exaltata

Tobacco plant
Nicotiana affinis
'Lime Green'
One of the few
garden plants with
green flowers.

Statice
Limonium sinuatum
Available in a
wide variety of
colours.

Hibiscus
Hibiscus syriacus 'Woodbridge'

Sweet sultan
Centaurea moschata

Prairie gentian
Eustoma grandiflorum

Gayfeather
Liatris callilepis
A very long-lived
cut flower, the
buds open from
the top down.

Clary
Salvia horminum

138

Monkshood
Aconitum napellus
Highly poisonous plants, monkshood should be handled with care.

The flowers of this plant are like lilac gypsophila and the leaves resemble maidenhair fern.

Meadow-rue
Thalictrum delavayi

Eryngium
Eryngium × oliverianum

Lily
Lilium 'Destiny'

Nectarine
Prunus persica 'Early Rivers'

African lily
Agapanthus Headbourne hybrid

Lily
Lilium auratum

Fernleaf yarrow
Achillea filipendulina

Tickseed
Coreopsis
If the stems are plunged into hot water after cutting, these brilliant yellow daisies last well in arrangements.

Mulberries
Morus nigra

Lavender
Lavandula angustifolia
A favourite cottage garden flower, with its silvery leaves and strongly scented flowers.

Everlasting pea
Lathyrus latifolius
The flowers of this perennial last well when cut.

139

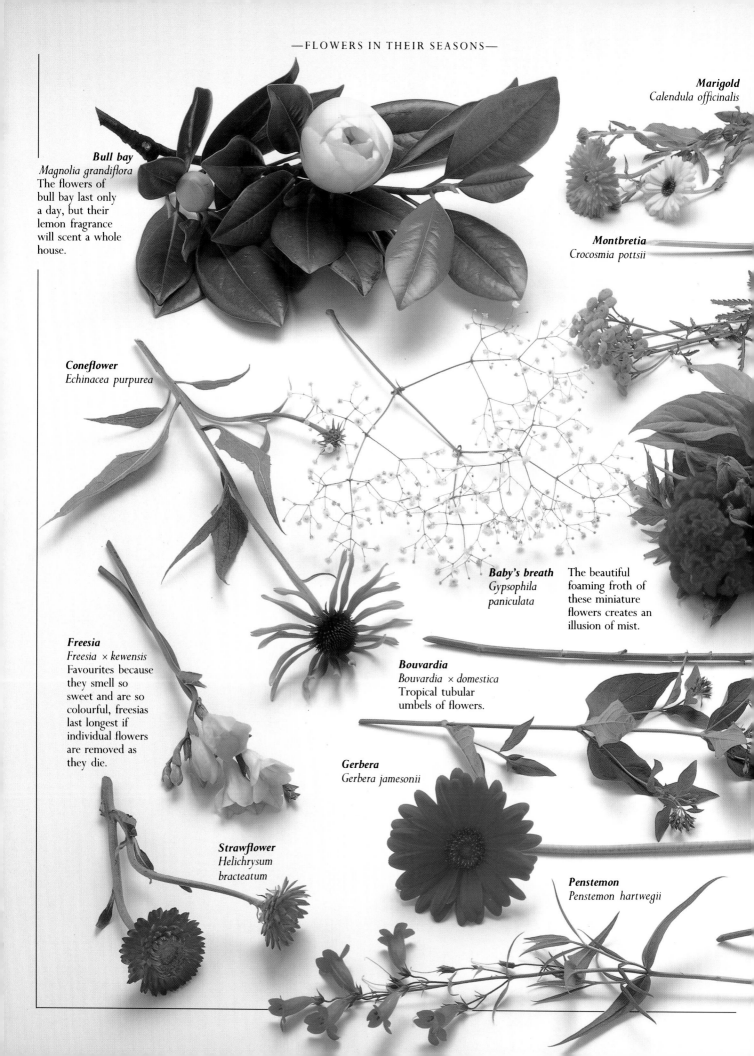

Bull bay
Magnolia grandiflora
The flowers of
bull bay last only
a day, but their
lemon fragrance
will scent a whole
house.

Marigold
Calendula officinalis

Montbretia
Crocosmia pottsii

Coneflower
Echinacea purpurea

Baby's breath
*Gypsophila
paniculata*
The beautiful
foaming froth of
these miniature
flowers creates an
illusion of mist.

Freesia
Freesia × kewensis
Favourites because
they smell so
sweet and are so
colourful, freesias
last longest if
individual flowers
are removed as
they die.

Bouvardia
Bouvardia × domestica
Tropical tubular
umbels of flowers.

Gerbera
Gerbera jamesonii

Strawflower
*Helichrysum
bracteatum*

Penstemon
Penstemon hartwegii

Phlox
Phlox paniculata

Honeysuckle
*Lonicera
periclymenum
serotina*

Tansy
Tanacetum vulgare

**Australian
honeysuckle**
Banksia menziesii
These robust sub-
tropical flowers make
a strong focal point.

Godetia
Clarkia grandiflora

Yellow horned-poppy
Glaucium flavum

Cockscomb
*Celosia argentea
cristata*

Opium poppy
Papaver somniferum

Double fringed pink
*Dianthus superbus
grandiflorus*

Peruvian lily
Alstroemeria ligtu
hybrid
These long-lasting
flowers are
available in a wide
colour range.

Black-eyed Susan
Rudbeckia hirta 'Double Gloriosa'

Carnation
Dianthus caryophyllus
'Scarlet Elegance'

Larkspur
Delphinium elatum
The pink, white
and blue spires of
larkspur last a
long while in
arrangements.

Larkspur
Delphinium elatum

Flowering currant
Ribes sanguineum

White poplar
Populus alba
The undersides of
the leaves of this
poplar shimmer a
brilliant silver in
an arrangement.

Barberry
Berberis thunbergii
'Rose Glow'

This variety of
barberry (above)
has plum-coloured
foliage, followed by
little red
berries.

Hebe
Hebe armstrongii

Caladium
Caladium × hortulanum

Spindle
Euonymus japonicus

Rose
Rosa glauca

Sword fern
Nephrolepis exaltata
Ferns are at their
best in mid-summer,
when the fronds have
hardened but have not
yet become damaged.

Artemisia
Artemisia ludoviciana

Cotton lavender
*Santolina
chamaecyparissus*

Wood spurge
Euphorbia amygdaloides

Senecio
Senecio 'Sunshine'

Plantain lily
Hosta fortunei
'Aureomarginata'
Leaf shape and
colour vary with the
variety of plantain
lily.

Jew's mallow
Kerria japonica

Bells of Ireland
Moluccella laevis
The brilliant green
spires of bracts
suit many
arrangements.

Lamb's tongue
Stachys byzantina

Fig
Ficus carica
Stems of these
leaves look
magnificent in
grand arrangements,
while single leaves
are effective in
smaller ones.

Rue
Ruta graveolens

Lady's mantle
Alchemilla mollis

Dogwood
Cornus alba
'Elegantissima'

—Arranging summer flowers—

*F*lowers of every hue fill the borders during the summer months, inspiring us to create colourful arrangements that will remain in the memory long after the warm sun has departed, reminding us of sunshine and clear blue skies.

Roses, paeonies, yarrow, larkspur, lavender and lilies; these are just a few of the flowers that look at their best in the more colourful containers that suit summer so well. Put away the muted greys, creams, white and browns of stoneware that are so appropriate for winter and spring arrangements and bring out the vases that feature sunny yellows, clear bright blues and brilliant greens; the glazed pots with splashes of red and ultramarine.

This is a good time of year to include in some of your arrangements the tender exotics that are available for most of the year in flower shops. Strelitzias, tuberoses and anthuriums all combine happily, but somewhat unusually, with herbaceous or hardy border plants, such as delphiniums and roses.

Create unusual and exciting effects by setting brilliant colours against one another. Try placing rich reds among lime-green foliage, pale lilac-pink next to burning orange, and lemon-yellow close to the brightest sky-blue. Of course, bright-coloured combinations are always a gamble but if you choose your flowers with confidence, such arrangements are almost bound to work well.

—PLANT MATERIAL—
'Carambole' roses, mare's tails, pink delphiniums, pink nerine and pale pink anthurium

*C*elebrate the arrival of summer with bright, lively arrangements. Every colour, form and texture of flower is available, so there is no excuse for dull arrangements!

—PLANT MATERIAL—
Wattle, cymbidiums, roses,
carnations, delphiniums,
amaryllis, elaeagnus, fatsia
and aucuba

The early summer sun warms this basket filled with the loveliest of flowers. The heady fragrance of the paeonies and sweet peas heightens the sensual pleasure.

—PLANT MATERIAL—
Delphiniums, paeonies, spurge, sweet peas, bridal wreath, whitebeam, cow parsley and corn marigolds

—PLANT MATERIAL—
Sunflowers

*T*hese two golden arrangements are very different in style. The huge sunflowers gaze proudly from a bulbous earthenware pot, while the array of pretty, wild-looking flowers has a light, wistful air.

—PLANT MATERIAL—
Blanket flowers, lady's mantle, cow parsley, tansies, ox-eye daisies and meadow grass

—PLANT MATERIAL—
'Louise Odier' roses

*F*ine china cups often make ideal containers for small-scale flower arrangements. The design will often suggest the flowers. Here, on the left, the old-fashioned 'Louise Odier' roses are identical to the rose motif, while the pale lemony-green on the Belleek cup below relates superbly to the frilly-edged variegated geranium leaf and the shape of the rose of Sharon.

—PLANT MATERIAL—
Geraniums, rose of Sharon, cigar plant, 'The Fairy' roses, corydalis, vervain, rose hips, mint and hyssop

—PLANT MATERIAL—
Foxgloves, blue
delphiniums, lilac
delphiniums and spurge

—PLANT MATERIAL—
Scabious, blue delphiniums,
carnations and Guelder rose
berries

*D*elphiniums are the main
ingredient in both these,
otherwise very different,
arrangements. On the far left,
a serene combination of
pastel-coloured foxgloves and
delphiniums stands coolly in
the crystal-glazed, grey-blue
vase. At left, a pink- and
blue-glazed jug fairly bursts
with glorious colour.

AUTUMN

irst signs of autumn are the heavy dews; at some stage in late summer, early in the morning, the grass will be covered with drops of water, making everything glisten and gleam. The weather can frequently be rather good in early autumn, but there is a brisk note in the air, and once again clothes need to be considered more for their properties of warmth. There seems to be a mellow quality everywhere. The rising and setting sun takes on deep golden colours, and the earth seems to have a new earthy scent. The clear, bright colours of summer now begin to give way to the warm autumnal rusts, oranges, golds and maroons that so perfectly match the winding down of plants before the rigours of winter. There is quite a long period in autumn when the change from summer seems fairly minimal and it is surprisingly late in the season when the leaves begin to turn colour before they fall.

This earlier part of the season is when the chrysanthemums come into their own. There are, of course, some relatives that flower in the summer, like *Leucanthemum maximum* with its large daisy flowers, but most chrysanthemums reserve their strength for a great autumn display. All the colours except blue are represented but there is a strong leaning towards the warm golden tones that we always associate with autumn. There are single, semi-double and double varieties of chrysanthemum, and they all have a sharp tangy smell, especially when their stems or leaves are crushed. I enjoy the smaller-flowered varieties much more than the large, ball-shaped, decorative and exhibition types which look like small cabbages on straight stems. These latter varieties are not nearly so easy to use in arrangements, as they are so rigid and formal. Their greatest attribute is that they last a long time once cut, unless they are accidentally knocked, when they can easily shatter altogether.

Flowers, fruit and foliage

Another plant that puts on a great show at this time of year is the dahlia. Its flowers are rather like chrysanthemums, but they are somehow crisper. The singles and pompons are the most attractive. Dahlias do not have the same long-lasting cut quality as chrysanthemums, although they have a reasonable life in water, particularly if they start with a drink of hot water. Other flowers that are at their best in early autumn are montbretia and scabious, and these are followed by nerines and kaffir lilies. The last of the lilies, the beautiful *Lilium speciosum*, flower at this time of year, too.

Autumn is the time when fruits ripen on the trees and in a good year branches are laden with rosy apples, deep red and yellow crab apples and golden pears. Crab apples look very attractive in flower arrangements, perhaps mixed with nerines, pompon dahlias and some decorative cabbage leaves.

The scarlet oak is one of the first trees to change colour, looking almost as if it is on fire. The chestnuts and maples soon follow suit and most trees and quite a few deciduous shrubs show some autumn colour for a couple of weeks. Liquidambar is another extremely well-coloured tree that turns a rich red, while the tulip tree takes on a strong yellow hue. Picked just as they are colouring, leaves will last for nearly a week in water, providing lovely indoor decoration. For the most effective display, simply arrange a cluster of autumn branches on their own in a plain earthenware vase.

Witch hazel
Hamamelis vernalis 'Sandra'

Black-eyed Susan
Rudbeckia hirta 'Goldilocks'

Tricolor chrysanthemums
Chrysanthemum carinatum
'Monarch Court Jester'

Scarlet oak
Quercus coccinea

Plants in **bold** type are shown on pp.156–163.
Acanthus mollis
Acer
Aesculus
Amaranthus caudatus
Amaryllis belladonna
Amelanchier canadensis
Anaphalis cinnamomea
Anemone × **hybrida**
Arbutus unedo
Aster novi-belgii
Berberis aggregata
Berberis thunbergii
Bouvardia × **domestica**
Callicarpa rubella
Callistemon
Callistephus chinensis

Capsicum annuum
Caryopteris × *clandonensis*
Castanea sativa
Cattleya labiata
Celastrus orbiculatus
Chrysanthemum
Cobaea scandens
Colchicum speciosum
Cosmos bipinnatus
Cotoneaster
Crocosmia
Cyclamen hederifolium
Dahlia
Erica vagans
Eucalyptus dalrympleana
Eucryphia × *nymansensis*
Euonymus europaeus
Fatsia japonica

Fothergilla monticola
Fuchsia
Gaillardia
Gentiana sino-ornata
Gladiolus
Gomphrena globosa
Hebe 'Autumn Glory'
Helenium autumnale
Helianthus annuus
Hydrangea
Hypericum elatum 'Elstead'
Iris foetidissima
Kniphofia
Kochia trichophylla
Leycesteria formosa
Liastris
Lilium speciosum
Liquidambar styraciflua

Malus sylvestris
Molucella laevis
Nerine bowdenii
Nerine flexuosa
Paphiopedilum venustum
Pernettya mucronata
Phygelius aequalis
Physalis alkekengi
Punica granatum
Pyrus communis
Rubus fruticosa
Rudbeckia
Schizostylis coccinea
Sedum
Sorbus
Typha latifolia
Viburnum opulus
Vitis vinifera

Fuchsias
Fuchsia 'Autumnale'

Scabious
Scabiosa columbaria

Cyclamen
Cyclamen hederifolium

Dahlias
Dahlia cv.

Acidanthera
Gladiolus callianthus

Similar in appearance to gladioli, this flower is sweet-scented at night.

Corn-on-the-cob
Zea mays

Strawberry tree
Arbutus unedo

Michaelmas daisy
Aster ericoides
'Monte Casino'

Chrysanthemum
Chrysanthemum
'Statesman'

Chrysanthemum
Chrysanthemum

Chrysanthemum
Chrysanthemum
'Evelyn Bush'
These large, stiff, incurving blooms are not easy to use.

Bear's breeches
Acanthus spinosus

Rose of Sharon
Hypericum calycinum
This plant can look weedy, but its flowers and stamens are beautiful.

Milkweed
Gomphocarpus

The seed pods of milkweed are low down on the stem, but the plant makes a bold shape in arrangements.

Statice
Limonium latifolium

Tickseed
Coreopsis
These daisies flower throughout the autumn. If the stems are placed in boiling water (see p.42) they will last well.

Dryandra
Dryandra sp.

Golden rod
Solidago
'Goldenmosa'
Much maligned as it grows so voraciously, the flowering spires are lovely.

Solanum
Solanum jasminoides album

Bouvardia
Bouvardia × *domestica*

Crab apple
Malus 'Yellow Siberian'
Colours range from black to yellow.

White snakeroot
Eupatorium sp.
With fluffy umbels of white flowers, the stems of white snakeroot should be plunged in boiling water before arranging.

Globe amaranth
Gomphrena globosa

Vervain
Verbena × hybrida

Pink nerine
Nerine bowdenii
Nerine grows best in a sunny position. Once cut, all the buds will open.

Scabious
Scabiosa caucasica
The flowers do particularly well in a good dry autumn, and the white variety is very beautiful.

Cup and saucer plant
Cobaea scandens

Flowering from early summer until well into the autumn, this climber has large flowers, varying from green to purple.

Lily
Lilium speciosum rubrum

With a sweet scent of toffee, these lilies last a long time.

Chinese gentian
Gentiana sino-ornata
Probably the most intense of all flower blues. Place in a light position.

Pale pink fuchsia
Fuchsia cv.
The flowers of fuchsias are not as fragile as they look.

Plume thistle
Cirsium japonicum
The stems of these flowers should be plunged in boiling water (see p.42) after cutting.

These long-lasting cornflower-like flowers dry easily in the vase.

Cupid's dart
Catananche caerulea 'Major'

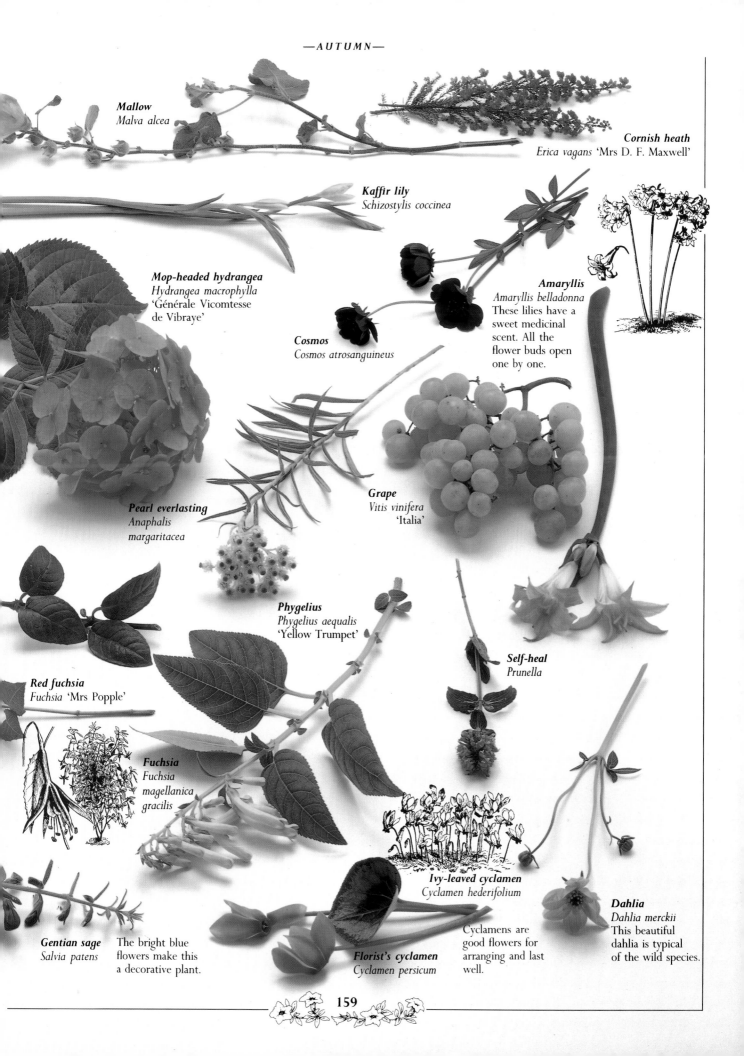

Mallow
Malva alcea

Cornish heath
Erica vagans 'Mrs D. F. Maxwell'

Kaffir lily
Schizostylis coccinea

Mop-headed hydrangea
Hydrangea macrophylla
'Générale Vicomtesse
de Vibraye'

Amaryllis
Amaryllis belladonna
These lilies have a
sweet medicinal
scent. All the
flower buds open
one by one.

Cosmos
Cosmos atrosanguineus

Grape
Vitis vinifera
'Italia'

Pearl everlasting
Anaphalis
margaritacea

Phygelius
Phygelius aequalis
'Yellow Trumpet'

Self-heal
Prunella

Red fuchsia
Fuchsia 'Mrs Popple'

Fuchsia
Fuchsia
magellanica
gracilis

Ivy-leaved cyclamen
Cyclamen hederifolium

Dahlia
Dahlia merckii
This beautiful
dahlia is typical
of the wild species.

Gentian sage
Salvia patens
The bright blue
flowers make this
a decorative plant.

Florist's cyclamen
Cyclamen persicum

Cyclamens are
good flowers for
arranging and last
well.

Love-lies-bleeding
Amaranthus caudatus

Love-lies-bleeding
Amaranthus caudatus
The great tassels
of maroon-
coloured flowers
are produced late
in the season.

Waratah
Telopea sp.

Chrysanthemum
Chrysanthemum indicum

Dahlia
Dahlia 'Nina Chester'

Love-lies-bleeding
Amaranthus caudatus

Chrysanthemum
Chrysanthemum
'Mason's Bronze'
These flowers are
the essence of
autumn,
particularly in the
rust, bronze and
maroon range
of colours.

Pepper
*Capsicum annuum
acuminatum*
'Friesdorfer'
These decorative
orange peppers
look attractive
with yellow and
red autumn
flowers.

China aster
Callistephus chiner

Michaelmas daisy
Aster novae-angliae
The delicate
fronds of daisy
flowers last well
until the frosts.

Chinese lantern
*Physalis alkekengi
franchetii*
The decorative
orange calyces
enclose the small
fruits.

160

Gladioli
Gladiolus nanus
'Peter Pears'

Gladioli
Gladiolus hortulanus

Ice plant
Sedum
'Autumn Joy'

Chrysanthemum
Chrysanthemum indicum

These spray
chrysanthemums
are available from
flower shops all
year round in
many varieties.

St John's wort
Hypericum inodorum
'Elstead'

Pitcher plant
Sarracenia sp.

China aster
*Callistephus
chinensis*
These long-lasting
flowers are available in
pink, red, lilac, cream
and white.

Windflower
Anemone × hybrida
'Honorine Jobert'

Chrysanthemum
Chrysanthemum indicum
'Charming'

Pomegranate
Punica granatum
The glowing skins
make these
extremely
beautiful to use.

Dryandra
Dryandra drummondii
These plants
produce exotic
flowers that last
well.

161

Snowdrop tree
Halesia monticola

Guelder rose
Viburnum opulus
The leaves of
many viburnums
turn a rich bronze,
although they
don't last long.

Horse chestnut
Aesculus sp.
The huge divided
leaves are attractive
when used in large
arrangements.

Stranvaesia
Photinia davidiana
An evergreen
shrub, or small
tree, which
produces a few
bright red leaves
amongst the green
ones throughout
the autumn.

Firethorn
Pyracantha coccinea
'Lalandei'

Berberis
Berberis thunbergii
atropurpurea
The leaves turn an
even richer purple
in autumn, but its
spines are no less
vicious.

Not only are rose
hips attractive to
use, they also
make a delicious
tea.

Rose hips
Rosa cv.

162

Forsythia
*Forsythia ×
intermedia*

Spindle
Euonymus europaeus

Sweet briar
Rosa eglanteria
Rose hips are very
decorative.

Crab apple
Malus × lemoinei

Strawberry tree
Arbutus unedo

Tulip tree
*Liriodendron
tulipifera*
A beautiful tree
with exotic light
green flowers.

Sweet gum
*Liquidambar
styraciflua*

Crab apple
Malus 'Profusion'
This variety has
bronze leaves in
summer and
autumn.

Scarlet oak
Quercus coccinea

163

Arranging autumn flowers

I love the autumn. Suddenly there is a cool, brisk feel to the early mornings, and colours everywhere seem to mellow. The bright, clear colours of summer soften and grow hazy, and gradually give way to the burning, glowing hues that seem absolutely right for the time of year when the leaves make their final display before falling prey to winter winds.

Gone are the white ox-eye daisies, but now in gardens there are a great range of dahlias, gladioli and hydrangeas, many of which are the colours of autumn. Chrysanthemums, too, although available all year round from flower shops, come into their own in the autumn. They can all look beautiful arranged simply in a plain vase or jug.

Of course, there are still some pink, white and blue flowers available but the general mood is of amber, rust, red, gold and brown. The sun, too, borrows these colours at this time of year, setting mistily in a rich orange ball like the heart of a great bonfire.

Autumn is full of wonderful smells: burning wood, leaves underfoot, and tangy chrysanthemums. Although there is not quite so much plant material around as in summer, arrangements can take on the look of rich tapestry.

Autumn is a great time for warm, natural looking containers: baskets and wooden pots, terracotta and pewter vases and warm-coloured ceramics. They should offset the warm colours of autumn flowers.

This glowing and colourful autumn arrangement would look sunny even in the darkest corner. An old terracotta pot makes an ideal container for this interesting mix of temperate and tender flowers, leaves and stems.

PLANT —MATERIAL— Chrysanthemums, Chinese lanterns, peppers, rowan, tea tree, flowering ivy, dryandra and proteas

Anemones are in good form in early autumn. They combine well with hydrangeas and contrast strongly with wheat, the texture of which is echoed by the wicker basket.

PLANT —MATERIAL— Anemones, hydrangeas and wheat

*G*lowing candles, berries, apples and flowers set in a copper bowl make a rich combination to display on a side table at a late autumn dinner party. The reds, oranges and pinks are accentuated by the rich, dark green foliage.

—PLANT MATERIAL—
**Kalanchoe plants,
Worcester apples, capsicum
berries, holly berries
and deodar branches**

*To make this vibrant
autumn arrangement,* set the
plants in one half of the bowl
and place two small plastic
bowls filled with wet foam in
the other half. Cut narrow
cylinders — slightly narrower
than the candles — into the
foam and push the candles
into each. Pile the apples
between the plastic bowls.
Insert the berried branches and
the foliage into the foam and
between the plants. Fill in any
gaps with moss.

*T*he lovely gold and rusty-pink pompon chrysanthemums, interspersed with trails of love-lies-bleeding, need to be set on a shelf so that the pink and green racemes of amaranthus flowers can be seen at their best advantage.

—**PLANT MATERIAL**—
Gold and rusty-pink pompon chrysanthemums and love-lies-bleeding

*T*he spiky green bud stems of
pale dusty-orange gladioli
poke jauntily above the brown
oak foliage. It is almost as
though they are looking back
at summer with their feet
planted firmly in autumn.

—PLANT MATERIAL—
Autumn oak and gladioli

Pink flowers are not usually
associated with this time of
year, but nerines flower well
into the autumn if grown in a
sheltered spot and speciosum
lilies flower late in the season.

—PLANT MATERIAL—
Nerines and speciosum
lilies

WINTER

Stripped of their remaining leaves, trees in winter look like gaunt and bony skeletons, and a greyness stretches over the countryside. At first sight it seems as if plants go into hibernation with the coming of winter. But if you look a little closer, it is amazing to see what continues to grow and flower. In the mild districts mahonias start to put up their sprays of flowerbuds in early winter, and if the weather is not too frosty, their yellow racemes of flowers open in mid-winter on sunny mornings. As a bonus, some of these have a scent of lily-of-the-valley, too. Another plant that flowers early in the winter is the evergreen *Fatsia japonica*, which produces heads of white flowers; however it is really its fig-like leaves that can look splendid in winter arrangements. There are several varieties of hellebore that flower in the winter, such as the Christmas rose, and the evergreen hellebore, which produces large heads of green flowers later in the season.

Fragrant flowering plants

One particular scented winter gem is wintersweet – *Chimonanthus praecox*. This is a deciduous wall shrub that looks quite ordinary for most of the year, but in mid-winter produces a crop of beautiful creamy, wax-like bells with a really strong fragrance. Unfortunately, it takes a few years to flower, but it is well worth a place in the garden, as a few flowering twigs brought inside will perfume a room for several days. Winter heliotrope is another winter-flowerer; it produces stems of delicate pink flowers with a honey-like scent, surrounded by almost circular leaves.

In late winter, witch hazel – *Hamamelis mollis* – grows strange, spidery, yellow flower petals with the most delicious scent. At the same time, the first bulbs, the winter aconites, produce their little, bright yellow flowers sur-rounded by a rosette of green leaves, and these are closely followed by the dainty snowdrops beloved by all. Both of these flowers will even push their way through the snow to produce their flimsy flowers on a sunny day.

Winter foliage

In addition to all the plants that magically produce their flowers in winter, there are the evergreen trees. Most of the conifers retain their foliage throughout the winter and these can look wonderful with their varied colours in an all-foliage arrangement. You can choose from junipers, cypresses, pines and cedars, yews and hemlocks. Each has many species with interesting colour variations: some are golden, some grey and some bluish-silver. Other evergreen shrubs, such as holly, have the advantage of producing bright red berries which persist until mid-winter or until the birds eat them. Mistletoe also produces berries in mid-winter – these are sticky and white but very decorative in arrangements. So, too, is ivy with its unusual panicles of seeds, and variegated leaves in silver and gold.

So winter is not quite as barren as it may at first appear and there are certainly plenty of opportunities to arrange foliage and flowers creatively. Of course, if you are unable to obtain many winter-flowering plants from your garden, there is always a wide range of all-year-round flowers that can be bought from a flower shop to supplement your own supplies.

Mahonia
Mahonia × media 'Charity'

Hellebore
Helleborus argutifolius

Bell heather
Erica carnea 'December Red'

Witch hazel
Hamamelis mollis 'Coombe Wood'

Plants in **bold** type are shown on pp.174–177.
Ananas
Anthurium
Arum italicum
Aucuba japonica
Azalea
Begonia rex
Bergenia
Betula pendula
Betula utilis
Bouvardia × domestica
Brassica
Buxus sempervirens
Camellia japonica
Capsicum
Cedrus
Chamaecyparis
Cichorium intybus

Cornus alba
Corylus avellana
Crocus
Cryptomeria japonica
Cupressus macrocarpa
Cyclamen coum
Cyclamen persicum
Daphne mezereum
Daphne odora
Eranthis hyemalis
Erica carnea
Eucalyptus
Euphorbia pulcherrima
Forsythia
Galanthus elwesii
Galanthus nivalis
Garrya elliptica
Hamamelis japonica
Hamamelis mollis

Hedera
Helleborus
Hippeastrum
Hyacinthus
Ilex aquifolium
Iris danfordiae
Iris histrioides
Iris reticulata
Iris unguicularis
Jasminum nudiflorum
Juniperus
Lachenalia
Larix leptolepis
Laurus nobilis
Lonicera fragrantissima
Mahonia
Narcissus 'February Gold'
Narcissus 'March Sunshine'
Odontoglossum

Picea
Pinus
Primula
Quercus ilex
Rhododendron
Salix
Skimmia japonica
Solanum capsicastrum
Strelitzia reginae
Symphoricarpos
Taxus baccata
Thuja
Tsuga
Tulipa
Viburnum farreri
Viburnum tinus
Vinca difformis
Viola
Viscum album

Snowdrops
Galanthus sp.

Holly
Ilex aquifolium 'Madame Briot'

Jasmine
Jasminum nudiflorum

Daphne
Daphne odora 'Aureo-marginata'

Daphne
Daphne odora
This plant produces
sweet-scented
flowers during mild
spells in winter.

Silk tassel bush
Garrya elliptica
Beautiful catkin
tassels trail from the
male plants in mid-
winter.

Heather
Erica × darleyensis
'Darley Dale'

Submerge the
branches in cold
water before
arranging (see p.41).

Euphorbia
Euphorbia fulgens

Wintersweet
*Chimonanthus
praecox*

The waxy, cream
bells of wintersweet
have the scent of
gardenias.

Primula
Primula obconica

Viburnum
*Viburnum ×
bodnantense*
These viburnum
flowers will perfume
a room for days.

Winter aconite
Eranthis hyemalis
The golden buds of
winter aconite open
in early winter.

Snowdrop
Galanthus nivalis

Witch hazel
Hamamelis mollis

These yellow
flowers have a clean
sharp scent.

Winter heliotrope
Petasites fragrans
Sweetly scented flowers grow from large, heart-shaped leaves in mid-winter.

Honeysuckle
Lonicera × purpusii
Perfumed creamy-white bell flowers make this plant ideal for winter arrangements.

Poinsettia
Euphorbia pulcherrima
Poinsettia stems should be sealed by burning them (see p.41) before arranging.

Hellebore
Helleborus argutifolius

The spiny leaves and rich green flowers last well when cut.

Laurustinus
Viburnum tinus
This evergreen viburnum produces flowers all winter.

Mahonia
Mahonia × media 'Charity'
These racemes of flowers smell of lily-of-the-valley.

Hellebore
Helleborus atrorubens

Iris
Iris danfordiae

Iris
Iris unguicularis

Winter jasmine
Jasminum nudiflorum

Elaeagnus
Elaeagnus pungens
'Maculata'
These leaves seem
to be splashed with
sunshine.

Senecio
Senecio 'Sunshine'

Griselinia
Griselinia littoralis
These waxy golden
green leaves last
well.

Yew
Taxus baccata

Hemlock
Tsuga canadensis

Cotoneaster
Cotoneaster
'Cornubia'

Camellia
Camellia japonica

Shallon
Gaultheria shallon
This plant forms
interestingly
shaped branches
of leaves.

Mahonia
Mahonia × media
'Charity'
Use single stems or
whole rosettes in
arrangements.

Mrs Robb's bonnet
*Euphorbia
amygdaloides
robbiae*

Skimmia
Skimmia japonica
The female plants
produce good
berries.

Portugal laurel
Prunus lusitanica

This tender shrub produces rich, shiny green leaves.

Southern beech
Nothofagus betuloides

Blue spruce
Picea pungens glauca
An excellent lasting blue conifer, ideal for winter arrangements.

Ivy
Hedera helix

Holly
Ilex aquifolium

Parchment-bark
Pittosporum tobira 'Variegatum'
This plant has beautifully variegated evergreen leaves.

Rosemary
Rosmarinus officinalis

Lawson's cypress
Chamaecyparis lawsoniana 'Lutea'

Fatsia
Fatsia japonica
These large dramatic leaves look especially good arranged with strong-coloured flowers.

——— *Arranging winter flowers* ———

*A*lthough winter is not the easiest time of year for flower arranging, there is nothing like a challenge, and just a few pieces of greenery combined with one or two flowers can look remarkably attractive. On the previous pages we have seen a few of the plants that produce flowers in the winter months, and these can all look delightful when arranged in even the smallest quantities. As we cannot sit in the garden simply enjoying it during this time of year, why not bring the garden inside by cutting a few bits and pieces for unusual arrangements in the house?

In the flower shops there are still quite a range of flowers available. There are carnations, chrysanthemums and freesias; spring flowers like narcissus, tulips, hyacinths and lilac; and a great range of exotic flowers such as lilies, gladioli and amaryllis from all over the world to give extra winter colour.

Both the low key garden arrangements and the more flashy-looking flower shop arrangements can cheer up a winter's week. It is a good time of year to use the rich, dark evergreen foliages of holly, yew and ivy, which will last for a long while once cut. They are lovely either by themselves or mixed with bright coloured flowers. I particularly like to place winter flowers in the more understated vases to reinforce the atmosphere of winter: subtle stoneware glazes in off-whites, greys and beiges, metal, stone and – of course – the ever-useful baskets.

*T*his low rustic basket of brilliantly coloured winter flowers would warm up the coldest of days.

—PLANT MATERIAL—
Lilies, amaryllis, broom, mimosa, poinsettia, skimmia, hyacinths and berried holly

This spiky winter twig arrangement is packed with richly scented, delicate flowers. These will all last well indoors if placed in a cool position.

—PLANT MATERIAL—
Witch hazel, wintersweet, viburnum, winter jasmine, winter honeysuckle and daphne

Rich green, spiky cryptomeria and berried cotoneaster with all the leaves removed cascade with larch twigs and cones from this mysterious, earthy pot.

**PLANT
—MATERIAL—
Cryptomeria, larch
twigs and cones and
cotoneaster**

*S*implicity is the keynote of these two striking flower arrangements, which use only three different sorts of plant material in all. The fans of mahonia with their star burst racemes of sweet-scented flowers (left) are arranged boldly and dramatically with sprigs of rosemary in a dark blue-green, faceted vase. The Christmas roses (above) stand out strongly against their dark green leaves in a simple vase.

Flowers for special occasions

Hardly a week of the year goes by without some sort of special occasion. It may be a friend's birthday, or a wedding anniversary, the birth of a baby or a small lunch party. Then there are all the high days and holidays such as Christmas and New Year's Day, Easter, and Thanksgiving. Flowers play an important part in all these festivities; they have been used as symbols of celebration through the ages by people from every country in the world. Whether the occasion is formal or informal, it will be made that much more comfortable by the presence of flowers. There is nothing like flowers for making us feel welcome.

For personal gifts, bear in mind the language of flowers and give a bunch that has a special meaning. It all adds a bit of mystery and, since a large proportion of the meanings attributed to flowers are happy and joyful, it is easy to find the right flowers to do the talking for you.

I like to keep the flower displays for special occasions very seasonal. It makes arranging flowers much more interesting and it makes everyone that much more intrigued by them. Now that it is possible to buy a wide range of flowers throughout the year, it is important to be selective and to choose flowers so that they suit their celebration and its season as closely as possible.

FLOWERS FOR GIVING

Flowers make an excellent present for every occasion. Every flower contains a message of transformation and growth, of joy and sunshine, so everyone loves to receive them. And flowers are so simple to give. Whether a pretty posy of flowers picked from the garden or made in a flower shop, an extravagant bouquet, or a container arrangement, a gift of flowers always gives immense pleasure. The very impermanence of flowers makes them all the more precious, a happy experience that can be stored away.

I am always saddened by those who say, "Oh no, I wouldn't give sweet peas as a present, they don't last two minutes; what about some spray chrysanthemums or some carnations?" Sweet peas are so marvellous: not only do they look beautiful, but they have an incredible scent. Everyone should be given sweet peas at least once a year no matter how short the time they last. Besides, spray carnations are available all year round, so you can give those when the sweet peas are not about.

Simple gifts replete with meaning

A posy, or all-round bunch of flowers, decorated with a bow makes an ideal present for a simple occasion. You might give a posy to your host or hostess at a lunch, coffee or tea party, or to say thank you for a helping hand, or to cheer up someone. A posy makes an ideal present to say, "I am thinking about you", and seems a highly appropriate present for a child to give. And it is easy to imbue your gift with special meanings. Give a red rose to say, "I love you", daisies for "innocence", some honeysuckle for "devoted affection", some ivy for "fidelity" and some tulips for "fame". To make the present and the message last a little longer all the recipient need do is pop the whole posy into a jug or mug after simply cutting the stems to the required length.

Wrapping and decoration

A bouquet makes a present that is a little more showy. They can be open or wrapped in cellophane, but they should always be decorated with a pretty bow. A bouquet is a special present to take to a dinner party, to give on Valentine's Day or Mother's Day, or in return for a very special favour. Choose your flowers carefully, combining colours that complement each other, and include some scented flowers in your bouquet to make it even more pleasurable to receive. Once removed from its wrapping the bouquet can be either arranged in a single vase, or split up and transformed into several smaller arrangements to be used around the house.

Grander floral gestures

Arrangements in containers are wonderful to receive. Whether they be affectionate little basket arrangements, middle-sized arrangements in pretty containers or large and opulent displays, they all make perfect presents for a special occasion like a birthday or anniversary, or for a festive occasion such as Christmas, Honneker, or the birth of a baby. Lovely container arrangements also make an ideal present for someone who is ill, either at home or in hospital. All the recipient need do to preserve the arrangement is top it up with water and it will give pleasure for days.

*B*irthday arrangements call for special vases. Here, the pastel-coloured flowers appear to spring out of a hastily opened parcel. Pink ribbon completes the overall effect, highlighting the lovely cornflowers.

**PLANT
—MATERIAL—
Snapdragons,
cornflowers and
statice**

Children love flowers, especially small flowers that are brightly coloured and cheerful-looking. Glowing reds and pinks, sunny yellows: it's the happy colours that they adore. Many little containers are ideal for simple flower arrangements for children to give. An egg cup, a little coffee cup or a cream jug are all ideal for children's arrangements. A posy, too, makes a delightful present for a child to give.

A few brightly coloured cyclamen flowers and some kaffir lilies look stunning in this terracotta jug.

This delicate sauce boat is made fragrant by setting mahonia flowers amongst silver Senecio 'Sunshine' foliage.

Egg shells sitting in egg cups make perfect little vases for a few multi-coloured polyanthus flowers.

Two sweetly scented roses, miniature white Michaelmas daisies and some fluffy mimosa make up this lovely posy.

This china basket makes a pretty little container for a group of red roses nestling in a bed of moss.

Small posies of flowers make perfect gifts for children to give. A nice idea is to use some sweet-scented flowers, like the hyacinths, broom and narcissus shown in these bunches.

Some garden marigolds and bright yellow statice with a few fern fronds make a sunny combination.

The delicacy of this mixture of pale pink broom mixed with hyacinths and white anemones is accentuated by the red bow.

Poppies are magic flowers especially when they are fully opened. Here they are mixed with gypsophila in a posy tied with a pale green bow.

Both the paperwhites and soleil d'or narcissus in this delightful spring posy smell deliciously sweet.

Valentine's Day

The celebration of St Valentine's Day as a day for lovers seems to have nothing to do with the actual St Valentine, a martyr who died on 14 February AD270. Instead it seems to have become confused with the ancient Roman feast of Lupercalia, where boys drew out the names of girls from a love urn.

Decorative Valentine's cards have been sent since the sixteenth century. These were often made with lace-edged paper and contained love poems. The practice of sending red roses is a relatively recent one, although the red rose has been a symbol of love since medieval times. Unfortunately the traditional bunch of red roses has now become very expensive around Valentine's Day; an alternative is to display a single red rose among a bouquet of other flowers.

As an alternative to a bunch of red roses, this Valentine's bouquet comprises a mixture of delicate white flowers, with one red rose nestling at its heart.

—PLANT MATERIAL—
Iceland poppies, stocks, gypsophila, euphorbia, white roses and red rose

A Valentine's gift with a red rose attached to the bow.

A heart-shaped basket is lined with sprigs of fern and then filled with miniature red roses and frothy sprays of gypsophila.

—PLANT MATERIAL—
Garnett roses, gypsophila and leather fern

—*Mother's Day & Golden Wedding*—

*M*other's Day and a golden wedding anniversary are two special occasions when flowers make lovely gifts. Giving a present for Mother's Day is a relatively new tradition, but of all the presents to choose from, flowers are the most popular. On this occasion, it is nice to give flowers that convey a message; as many of the meanings from the language of flowers are to do with the pleasant things of life, it is not difficult to find a combination of flowers that look beautiful together, and at the same time convey some feelings about your relationship with your mother.

You could make a bouquet of roses, meaning "love", with stocks for "lasting beauty", and gillyflowers for "bonds of affection". Or you could combine yellow lilies meaning "gaiety", with red chrysanthemums for "I love" and daffodils for "regard". Other appropriate flowers are bluebells meaning "constancy", and red tulips as a "declaration of love".

For a golden wedding anniversary the colour of the flowers you give is often more important than their meanings, and there are lots of golden and yellow flowers to choose from.

Both bouquets and arrangements of flowers make popular presents and in each case the presentation is all important. A bouquet needs to be crisply wrapped in cellophane with a bow that matches the flowers, while an arrangement should be carefully made with an eye on its composition, and prettily beribboned.

*T*his pretty basket of flowers makes a perfect Mother's Day gift. The white roses are a sign of love while daisies are a symbol of patience.

—PLANT MATERIAL—
White roses, daisies and irises

—PLANT MATERIAL—
Yellow roses and wattle

A golden wedding anniversary is an important one, marking 50 years of marriage. The occasion is often marked by a party, and the colour of the flowers you give is all important. There are lots of golden-coloured flowers you can use, from yellow roses and chrysanthemums, to the more exotic lilies; you can make either a simple bouquet (left) or a more elaborate arrangement (below). You could also celebrate other wedding anniversaries, such as ruby or emerald, with gifts of colour-linked flowers.

—PLANT MATERIAL—
Yellow lilies, golden euphorbia, yellow freesias, chrysanthemums, dahlias, crab apples and privet

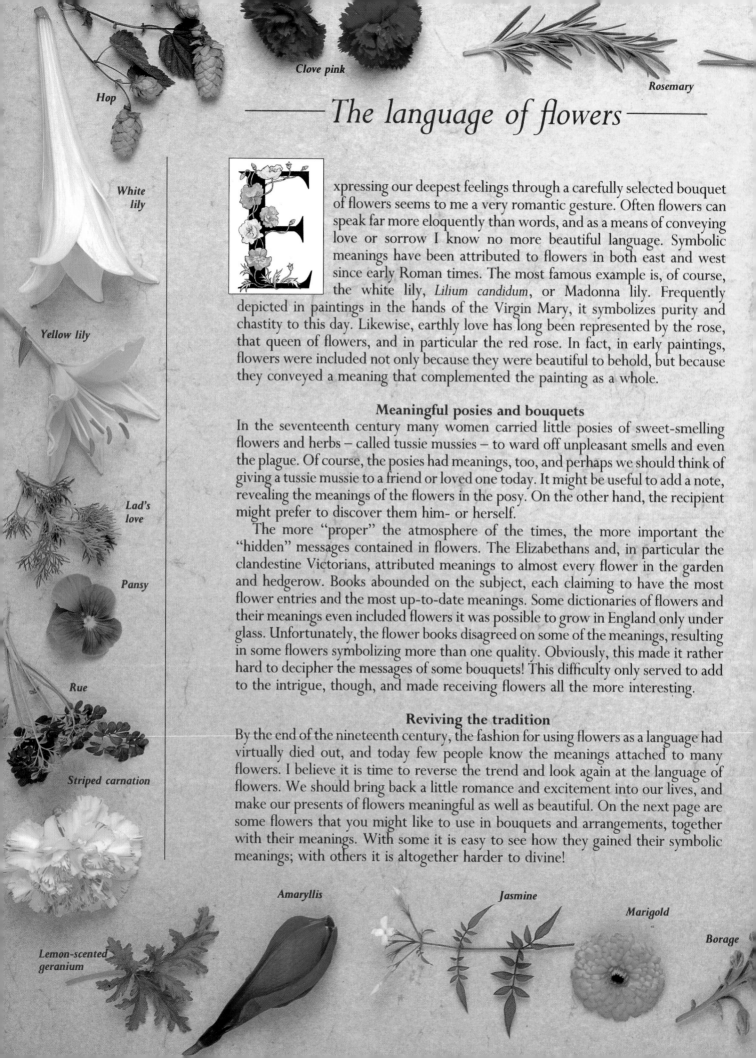

The language of flowers

Hop

Clove pink

Rosemary

White lily

Yellow lily

Lad's love

Pansy

Rue

Striped carnation

Lemon-scented geranium

Amaryllis

Jasmine

Marigold

Borage

Expressing our deepest feelings through a carefully selected bouquet of flowers seems to me a very romantic gesture. Often flowers can speak far more eloquently than words, and as a means of conveying love or sorrow I know no more beautiful language. Symbolic meanings have been attributed to flowers in both east and west since early Roman times. The most famous example is, of course, the white lily, *Lilium candidum*, or Madonna lily. Frequently depicted in paintings in the hands of the Virgin Mary, it symbolizes purity and chastity to this day. Likewise, earthly love has long been represented by the rose, that queen of flowers, and in particular the red rose. In fact, in early paintings, flowers were included not only because they were beautiful to behold, but because they conveyed a meaning that complemented the painting as a whole.

Meaningful posies and bouquets

In the seventeenth century many women carried little posies of sweet-smelling flowers and herbs – called tussie mussies – to ward off unpleasant smells and even the plague. Of course, the posies had meanings, too, and perhaps we should think of giving a tussie mussie to a friend or loved one today. It might be useful to add a note, revealing the meanings of the flowers in the posy. On the other hand, the recipient might prefer to discover them him- or herself.

The more "proper" the atmosphere of the times, the more important the "hidden" messages contained in flowers. The Elizabethans and, in particular the clandestine Victorians, attributed meanings to almost every flower in the garden and hedgerow. Books abounded on the subject, each claiming to have the most flower entries and the most up-to-date meanings. Some dictionaries of flowers and their meanings even included flowers it was possible to grow in England only under glass. Unfortunately, the flower books disagreed on some of the meanings, resulting in some flowers symbolizing more than one quality. Obviously, this made it rather hard to decipher the messages of some bouquets! This difficulty only served to add to the intrigue, though, and made receiving flowers all the more interesting.

Reviving the tradition

By the end of the nineteenth century, the fashion for using flowers as a language had virtually died out, and today few people know the meanings attached to many flowers. I believe it is time to reverse the trend and look again at the language of flowers. We should bring back a little romance and excitement into our lives, and make our presents of flowers meaningful as well as beautiful. On the next page are some flowers that you might like to use in bouquets and arrangements, together with their meanings. With some it is easy to see how they gained their symbolic meanings; with others it is altogether harder to divine!

Lily-of-the-valley

Lavender

Fennel

Red rose

Sweet pea

Heather

Fuchsia

Alyssum Worth beyond beauty
Amaryllis (*Hippeastrum*)
Splendid beauty
The great trumpet flowers are magnificent.
Anemone Forsaken
Angelica Soaring thoughts
Apple Temptation
Adam and Eve were the first to be tempted.
Aster I partake your sentiments
Azalea Temperance
Batchelor's buttons Celibacy
Bay Glory
Used in heroes' garlands.
Bear's breeches The fine arts
Belladonna lily (*Amaryllis belladonna*) Pride, silence
Bluebell Constancy
Borage Courage
Cabbage Profit
Red camellia Unpretending excellence
White camellia Perfect loveliness
Red carnation Alas for my poor heart
Striped carnation Refusal
Yellow carnation Disdain
Pink cherry tree Good education
Christmas rose Scandal, calumny
Red chrysanthemum I love you
White chrysanthemum Truth
Yellow chrysanthemum Slighted love
Clematis Mental beauty
Columbine Folly
Convolvulus Fleeting joy
These beautiful flowers last a very short time.
Crocus Youthful gladness
The first sign of spring.
Cyclamen Diffidence
Daffodil Regard
Dahlia Pomp
Dahlias are very grand and brilliantly coloured flowers.
Daisy Innocence
Fennel Flattery
Fig Idleness

Forget-me-not True love
These little blue flowers were often planted beside graves.
Foxglove Insincerity
Fuchsia Taste
Lemon-scented geranium Unexpected meeting
Gilliflower Bonds of affection
Heather Solitude
Heather is often seen growing on isolated mountainsides.
Hollyhock Ambition
Honesty Honesty
Honeysuckle Generous affection
This flower spreads its delicious scent generously.
Hop Injustice
Hyacinth Game sport
Hyssop Sacrifice
Ice plant Your looks freeze me
Iris Message
Ivy Fidelity
Because of its clinging growth, ivy has to be faithful to its host.
Jasmine Amiability
Jonquil I desire a return of affection.
Lad's love Jest
Larkspur Infidelity
Lavender Distrust
Lilac First emotions of love
Regal lily Majesty
What could be more regal?
White lily Purity
Yellow lily Falsehood
Lily-of-the-valley Return of happiness
Its sweet-scented bells open just at the beginning of spring.
Love-in-a-mist Perplexity
Magnolia Love of nature
Marigold Grief
Michaelmas daisy Afterthought
These pretty daisy flowers bloom into late autumn.
Mimosa Secret love
Mint Wisdom
Mock orange Counterfeit
Resembles the true orange.
Mulberry I shall not survive you
Myrtle Love
Nasturtium Patriotism

Pansy Thoughts
Parsley Rejoice
Phlox Unanimity
Pineapple You are perfect
Clove pinks Resignation
Red pinks Pure love
Striped pinks Refusal
Polyanthus Pride of riches
The flowers open with an array of bright, rich colours.
Red poppy Consolation
Scarlet poppy Fantastic extravagance
White poppy Sleep
Primrose Early youth
One of the earliest spring flowers.
Raspberry Remorse
Rhododendron Danger
Red rose Love
From earliest times, the rose has been associated with love.
White rose I am worthy of you
Yellow rose Jealousy
Full-blown rose concealing two buds Secrecy
Rosemary Remembrance
Rue Grief
Scabious Unfortunate love
Snapdragon Presumption
Stock Lasting beauty
Flowers over a long period.
Sunflower Haughtiness
Sweet pea Departure
Once cut, the sweet pea is extremely short-lived.
Sweet william Gallantry
Thyme Activity
Tuberose Dangerous pleasures
Its heady, delicious scent can almost make you faint.
Tulip Fame
Red tulip Declaration of love
Yellow tulip Hopeless love
Violet Modesty
Violets hide their flowers beneath their leaves.
Water lily Purity of heart
Weeping willow Mourning
Its drooping branches and leaves look like tears.
Yarrow War

Poppy

Larkspur

Nasturtium

Parsley

FLOWERS FOR WEDDINGS

The wedding ceremony is one of the most important ceremonies of our lives and because of this, the event can be rather over-whelming. However, amid all the formality of the occasion, flowers can provide the informal element, emanating a sense of ease and well-being. So for a wedding, it is well worth making that extra effort when creating beautiful arrangements.

The bride usually carries a bouquet of flowers, and this can take a variety of forms, ranging from a simple bunch of garden flowers to a much more elaborate bouquet where the flowers are wired so that they can overflow in a delicate shower of blooms and foliage. The style and colours of the flowers used all depend on the type of wedding and the design of the bride's dress. A bunch of lilies can make a wonderfully elegant bouquet to be carried in the crook of the bride's arm, or for a more informal wedding, a simple posy can be just the right accessory.

Then there are the flowers for the bride's hair. Again, they can be just simple single flowers pinned into position, or a circlet or half-circlet of flowers that garland the bride's head.

Bridesmaids, too, usually carry flowers. They can have similar flowers to the ones the bride carries, although it is more usual for bridesmaids to carry small posies of flowers rather than a shower bouquet. If they are small children, they can carry little baskets or small hoops of flowers, or maybe even a pretty ball of flowers hanging from a ribbon. The bridesmaids' flowers should complement the colour and style of their dresses, but at the same time relate to the bride's flowers so that the whole ensemble looks perfect.

Preparing the flowers

All the flowers that are carried or worn at a wedding have to be prepared only a short while before the ceremony as they will soon begin to wilt. Before arranging them, it is best to give them a good, long drink of water. Carnations and spray carnations, single chrysanthemums, freesias, Peruvian lilies, stephanotis, gypsophila and half-open roses all last quite well and can be prepared up to 12 hours in advance, so long as they are then kept in a cool place. It is not a good idea to keep them in the refrigerator, however, as this is *too* cold and the flowers can easily become frosted. Flowers such as sweet peas, full blown roses, Christmas roses and lilies-of-the-valley are more short-lived so they need to be prepared much nearer the time.

Decorating the church

Just as important as the flowers for the bride and groom are the flowers that decorate the church. It looks lovely if these can echo the colours of the bride's flowers, but it is important to bear in mind that churches are not always the most brightly lit places, and so often either very pale or very brightly coloured flower arrangements will look best.

There are usually two substantial flower arrangements made for inside the church, one on either side of the altar, that can be seen from every position. It is also a nice idea to have an arrangement near the entrance which will welcome everyone as they come in. Window ledges can also be decorated, pillars can be garlanded and arrangements can also be made for the pew ends.

This window-ledge arrangement for a church wedding echoes the garland of old-fashioned cottage flowers depicted in the stained glass window behind. The ribbed terracotta bowl adds to its feeling of simplicity.

—**PLANT MATERIAL**—
Single and pompon
chrysanthemums, ice plant,
snapdragons, ferns and
Cupid's dart

Spring weddings

Spring is the time when everyone's thoughts traditionally turn to love, and indeed it is the most popular time for getting married. There is a wide choice of flowers you can use for spring wedding bouquets, posies and arrangements, to suit both formal and more informal ceremonies.

For a grand white wedding, simple arrangements using only white flowers look most suitable, adding to the formality of the occasion. Alternatively, for a more informal wedding ceremony, combinations of pastel colours – pale blue, cream, ice pink, apricot, peach and lilac – can look fresh and appealing. These colours are represented by such flowers as roses, spray carnations, orchids, freesias, grape hyacinths and single hyacinths, all of which are available in flower shops in spring.

A garland of pastel-coloured flowers can be used to decorate a buffet table, to encircle the wedding cake, or they can even be twisted prettily around the poles that support a marquee. Trailing smilax is the easiest foliage to use, intertwined with wired bunches of flowers.

PLANT —MATERIAL—
Cream and pink miniature roses, heather, marguerites and smilax

In this French wedding cake decoration, flowers tumble prettily from a raised bowl, and cover the top of the cake.

Making the bouquet

—PLANT MATERIAL—
7 stems lily-of-the-valley, 4 heather sprigs, 3 orchids, 15 stephanotis flowers, 5 rosemary sprigs, 6 ivy stems, 5 stems of larkspur, 10 senecio stems, 6 white roses and 9 fern fronds

Before you assemble this all-white bride's bouquet, first wire all the ingredients individually (see p.44).

Then start to make the trail. Bind some ferns, small flowers and foliage together with fine-gauge reel wire.

Wire in more flowers to make the triangular shape.

Although this bouquet is time-consuming to make, the end result looks sumptuous and fresh with its sparkling white flowers and silver and green foliage; it also has a delightful, fresh perfume.

Cover all the wire with gutta-percha tape as you proceed. Bend the flowers at 90° to the stems, to form the handle.

Add the remainder of the material, and bind the wires at the top of the handle, near the bend.

When you have spread the flowers attractively, bind the bouquet handle tightly with white ribbon.

Wrap the ribbon down the handle, then back up again. Tie the ends together ready to attach a trailing bow.

—PLANT MATERIAL—
**Miniature cream and pink
roses, statice, leather fern
and heather**

A *basket of delicate little
flowers looks very pretty and
is ideal for a young
bridesmaid to carry. The
colours of the flowers should
complement the colour of
the bridesmaid's dress.*

To decorate this hair comb,
*cover a piece of medium-gauge
stub wire, 4cm (2in) longer
than the comb, with gutta-
percha tape. Tie a bunch of
flowers to the wire. Cover the
wire with tape, then wire on
two more bunches of flowers to
overlap the first. Bend the
wired flowers into the comb.*

*O*rchids are favourite flowers for weddings. Here, one is wired with a spray of camellia leaves for an elegant decoration.

—**PLANT MATERIAL**—
Cream and pink roses, smilax and laurustinus

To make a flowery ball, cut out a sphere-shape in foam and soak it in water. Double over a piece of heavy-gauge stub wire and push it through the foam sphere. Bend the two ends back to secure in place. Attach a ribbon to the wire loop and hang the ball up. Then fill it with some flowers and foliage to cover the foam. Finally attach a bow to the ribbon.

A spray of freesias with tellima foliage looks bright and fresh for wearing at a wedding. So, too, does the peach rose with eucalyptus leaves. The white rose makes a simple, yet classic buttonhole for a man to wear.

Summer weddings

Summer is the most wonderful time of year for a wedding. Flowers are at their best and most colourful. Early summer flowers include paeonies in red, pink and white, and wonderful roses. Both these flowers can look sumptuous in the church or reception arrangements as well as in bouquets.

Then there are sweet peas with their delicious scent. A bride's bouquet of these delicate, fragrant flowers is so special. They are not easy to wire and this job must be done at the last moment, but they are well worth both the time and trouble. Wild-looking bunches comprising sweet peas, mock orange, rosemary (for remembrance) and some silvery foliage are also excellent for the bride and bridesmaids. These

flowers look beautiful worn on the head either as a circlet or as little groups of flowers pinned into the hair. Circlets with a twiggy base are pretty to hold, either for the bride or her bridesmaids.

As the summer progresses, there are so many colours to choose from: intense blues, pinks, clear yellows and oranges, not forgetting white, like the white of cow parsley, gypsophila and, my favourite, lilies.

Try to relate the flowers for the church and reception with the hand flowers for the bride and bridesmaids, either by using the same colours, or the same flowers. Have no fear about creating a rich *mélange* of colours. A colourful mixture of flowers seems to be absolutely appropriate throughout the summer.

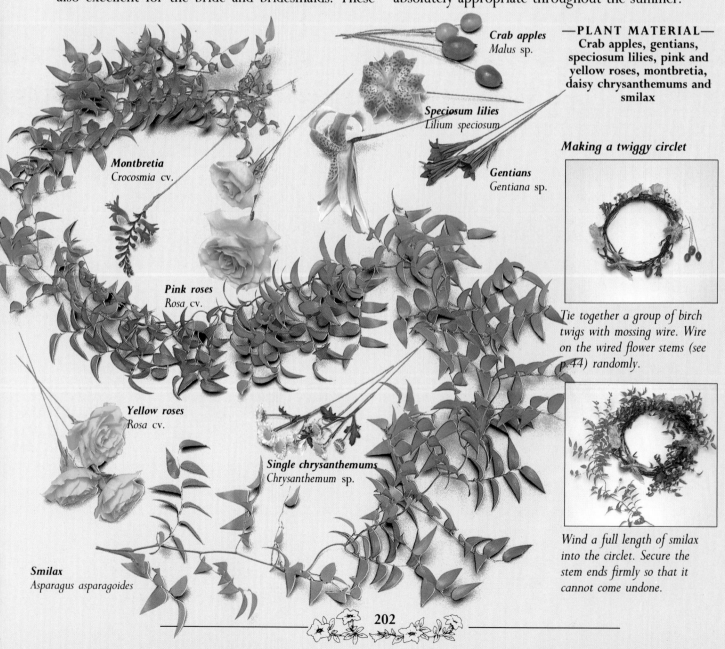

Crab apples
Malus sp.

Speciosum lilies
Lilium speciosum

Gentians
Gentiana sp.

Montbretia
Crocosmia cv.

Pink roses
Rosa cv.

Yellow roses
Rosa cv.

Single chrysanthemums
Chrysanthemum sp.

Smilax
Asparagus asparagoides

—**PLANT MATERIAL**—
Crab apples, gentians, speciosum lilies, pink and yellow roses, montbretia, daisy chrysanthemums and smilax

Making a twiggy circlet

Tie together a group of birch twigs with mossing wire. Wire on the wired flower stems (see p.44) randomly.

Wind a full length of smilax into the circlet. Secure the stem ends firmly so that it cannot come undone.

*P*ew ends provide a glowing welcome for guests. The flowers will last well because they are fixed in wet foam. Bouquets could also be hung, but they would have to be made at the last minute to ensure that they remain fresh looking throughout the ceremony.

—PLANT MATERIAL—
Decorative cabbage, speciosum lily, montbretia, Michaelmas daisies, fennel, berberis, larkspur, yellow roses and beech foliage

Making a pew end

Using a wet, foam-filled frame as a base, fix a cabbage at the top centre. Insert the shorter-stemmed flowers around it, filling in at the back.

Add the longer-stemmed lily, monbretia and foliage to trail almost to the floor.

—PLANT MATERIAL—
Decorative cabbage, gentians, pink, yellow and peach roses, Michaelmas daisies, speciosum lily, montbretia and larkspur

Making a bouquet

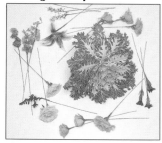

Wire the flower stems individually (see p.44). You will need only a few of each type of flower.

Insert the wired stems into the cabbage. Make sure that the wires run parallel and close to the cabbage stem.

Wind a piece of ribbon from the top to the bottom of the wires and back again.

Tie a bow (see p.47) just below the flower-heads.

Delicate, yet brightly coloured, this matching circlet and posy would look wonderful with most dress fabrics. Although it is somewhat unusual to walk down the aisle holding a cabbage, in fact its leaves are very beautiful and make a perfect foil for the flowers.

CELEBRATIONS THROUGH THE YEAR

Life would be extremely boring if there were no special occasions to enjoy. Fortunately there are many reasons to celebrate throughout the year, and these special occasions act as welcome punctuation points, making sense of the words and deeds in between. Flowers can play a large part in all these occasions, for flowers are a celebration in themselves. At the very beginning of the year there is New Year's Day, the day when everything starts afresh and there is much play on making New Year's resolutions and turning a new leaf. This is a day when it is good to give a quiet lunch or dinner party to welcome in the new year. As there are not very many flowers growing in gardens, now is the time to buy flowers from your local flower shop to create fresh and colourful arrangements to brighten the dinner table and living room.

Valentine's Day is the next occasion to celebrate. This is when a present of flowers – especially red roses – to the one you love is the order of the day.

Spring and summer

The most important festival in the Christian calendar is Easter, the date of which varies from year to year although it is always in spring. At this time of year the churches are decorated with arrangements of Easter lilies, with their great, white trumpets and soft, sweet scent. It is the time, too, for decorating eggs and making a flowery Easter nest.

May Day and Midsummer's Day follow soon after. At this time of year, there is an abundance of flowers you can gather from the garden and use in flower arrangements throughout the house. If the weather is good enough, a wonderful way to relax is to have an al fresco dinner party on a balmy evening, when the scents of summer flowers will gently perfume the air.

Autumn and winter

In September comes the Jewish New Year, a time for giving presents of flowers in the form of beautiful arrangements and bouquets. With the ripening of the crops comes Harvest Festival and, later in the year, on the fourth Thursday of November, the Americans celebrate their day of Thanksgiving. For these autumnal celebrations, wonderful arrangements can be made using striking combinations of fruit and foliage, in addition to flowers.

The countdown to Christmas Day begins in November with the four weeks of Advent. In many countries this period is celebrated with a wreath containing four candles, one being lit on each Sunday of the month. You can make an Advent wreath with fresh flowers and foliage and renew it each week. Even at the beginning of Advent the decorations are in evidence for Christmas. This is the one celebration of the year when most entertaining is done, and there are lots of Christmas tree decorations, berried holly garlands for the front door and wonderful arrangements of flowers, fruit and candles for the dinner table and living room that can be made.

The end of the year signals the final celebration of the year – New Year's Eve – and then the next year of celebrations begins.

Each one of these occasions can be celebrated with flowers, and as they cover all the seasons of the year, there can be a wealth of variation of flowers and foliage in the arrangements you create.

This elegant arrangement of pure white Easter lilies mixed with pussy willow, in a lustrous square-sided vase, will last extremely well, especially if it is situated in the cool of a church. The lilies have a sweet and delicate perfume that is softer than many other lilies.

—PLANT MATERIAL—
**Easter lilies and pussy
willow**

*E*aster is the most important festival in the Christian calendar, when all the churches are decorated with flowers. To decorate your home, and for a festive change – one that children will love – why not make a flowery Easter nest using the spring flowers available in your garden and some hand-painted eggs.

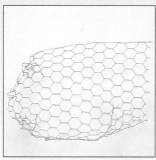

To make the nest, first cut out a rectangle from a piece of chicken-wire using wire cutters. Then fold the corners over and tuck them in to form a neat nest shape.

Thread a stub wire needle with raffia, and then use it to sew clumps of hay and a few alder catkin twigs on to the wire frame as neatly as possible to form the nest.

Line the nest with a sheet of plastic, or any other water-holding container, and fill this base with wet foam. Arrange the flowers and painted eggs in the foam.

—PLANT MATERIAL—
Flowering currant, polyanthus, single chrysanthemums, orchids, Cape cowslips and alder catkins

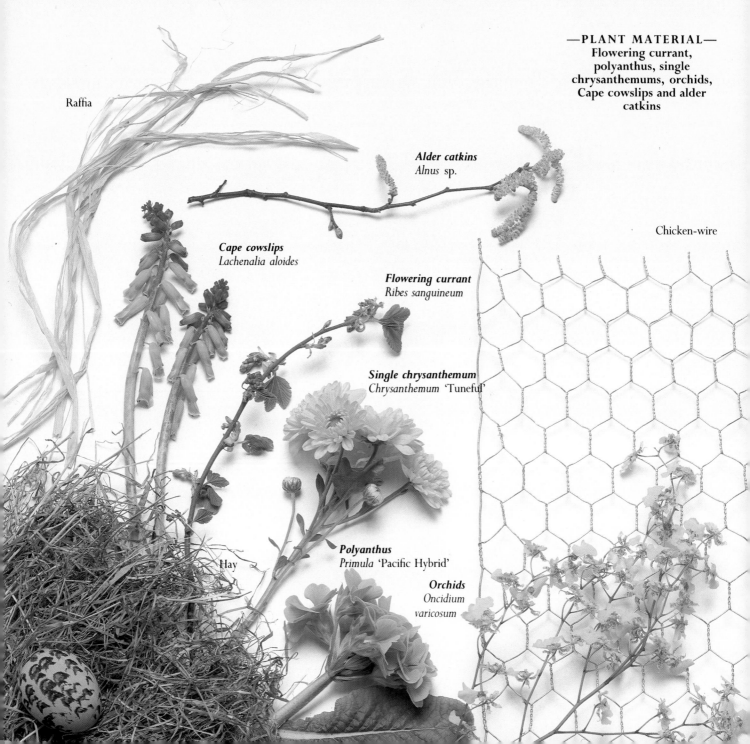

Raffia

Alder catkins
Alnus sp.

Chicken-wire

Cape cowslips
Lachenalia aloides

Flowering currant
Ribes sanguineum

Single chrysanthemum
Chrysanthemum 'Tuneful'

Hay

Polyanthus
Primula 'Pacific Hybrid'

Orchids
Oncidium varicosum

*T*his sunny Easter nest
displays a mixture of glowing
yellow, pink and fresh green
flowers and foliage
surrounding a cluster of
painted eggs that echo the
colours of the arrangement.
Any combination of spring
flowers can be used to achieve
this informal look.

Harvest thanksgiving

With autumn comes the ripening of many crops: cereals, apples, pears, pomegranates, persimmons and melons, nuts and grapes, artichokes and sweet corn, pumpkins and multi-coloured peppers. Churches are laden with the fruits of the harvest: even those in the cities manage to have wondrous displays of gold and rust and yellow. These colours are echoed by the many varieties of chrysanthemum and dahlia, strawflower and gladioli that flower in profusion at this wonderful time of year.

The celebration of the harvest is one of the most ancient of all festivals, dating from pagan times when communities were dependent on the success of their own crops. Today, we are not nearly so aware of the quality of the harvest. Even after a very wet and sunless summer, when the farmers have been complaining that the harvest will be poor, there are still bountiful supplies of harvest fruits and vegetables in the shops.

Harvest thanksgiving is a time to celebrate at home and to reflect on the effects of the seasons on our lives. What better way to do this than to give a thanksgiving party with harvest decorations. Arrangements look splendid in glowing autumn colours: rich amber, sunny gold and nutty brown. Make the fruits, vegetables and cereals an integral part of your harvest arrangement, perhaps created for a thanksgiving table display, or incorporate them in some rich garlanding to be placed around a doorway or buffet table.

A small, hollowed-out pumpkin lined with plastic forms the container for this autumnal arrangement. The late sunshine colours of foliage, berries and flowers make this a happy, sympathetic combination.

—PLANT MATERIAL—
Spindle, snowberries, Chinese lanterns and yellow and rust strawflowers

—PLANT MATERIAL—
Damp moss, 'Destiny' lilies,
rose hips, Worcester
apples, red and yellow
peppers, chilli peppers, box
foliage, barley, old man's
beard and eucalyptus seeds

Making a robust garland

*G*arlands are ideal
for decorating a
doorway, fireplace,
table, niche or
painting. If you wish
to make a long
garland, join together
individual moss-filled,
chicken-wire tubes
with mossing wire,
and cover with more
wired plant material.

*First wire the peppers,
apples and lilies (see
p.44). Then cut a
strip of chicken-wire
to the length and
width that you require
the garland to be. Pile
damp moss all along
the centre of the
chicken-wire and roll
it into a firm tube.*

*Taking one section of
the tube at a time,
poke the stems and
wires of the
ingredients into the
moss. Make sure the
flowers lie in the
direction in which the
garland will
eventually hang.
Overlap the material
so that the wire base
cannot be seen.*

*T*his thanksgiving table is laden with seasonal arrangements, using flowers, fruits, cereals and vegetables: a conventional arrangement in a glass vase, a glowing basket of fruit and vegetables, a bundle of long-eared wheat tied with a plaited raffia rope and a delicate garland of autumnal flowers. In addition, an apple and pear have been rather imaginatively used as containers for little flowers. The arrangements could equally well be used separately on side tables, sideboards, shelves and window sills.

—PLANT MATERIAL—
Wavy nerine, Guernsey nerine, apricot and peach roses, laurustinus and carnations

—PLANT MATERIAL—
Ivy, rust, orange and pink
chrysanthemums,
carnations, white nerine,
laurustinus and berried
holly twigs

Making a wired garland

Wire all the ingredients (see
p.44), except the ivy, to
strengthen the stems and make
them more flexible.

Select a small group of flowers
and wire them together, using
mossing or reel wire. This
makes the process quicker.

Cover the stems of the bunch
with gutta-percha tape (see
p.45). Make up
another bunch and
wire to the first.

Continue until the garland is
the length you require.
Entwine trails of ivy around
the flowers to complete.

Christmas

There has been a mid-winter festival since early pagan times, when boughs of evergreen, including mistletoe, conifer, holly and ivy, were brought into the house. In the fourth century, Christmas – the word is derived from Christ's Mass – was first celebrated by the Church and gradually the pagan and Christian festivals became merged. The exchanging of presents was a pre-Christian tradition; so too was the custom of having lanterns in the house, which today take the form of Christmas tree lights. The Christmas tree is quite a recent addition to the celebrations, made popular by Prince Albert, who imported large numbers of them from his estate in Coburg in 1845. Flowers and evergreen foliage now play a large part in our Christmas festivities. Christmas trees are sold in their millions and it is exciting to decorate the house with some beautiful flower arrangements and some garlanding. Flower shops can supply a wide range of colourful and long-lasting flowers, as well as the familiar holly, mistletoe, ivy and pine tree branches.

I love the more traditional Christmas arrangements and decorations: a Christmas tree simply decorated a few days before Christmas with candles and bows; a wreath of holly and pine for the front door; some rich garlanding; and some arrangements in glowing colours, perhaps with candles, to brighten the hallway, living room, sideboard or the dinner table. They are part of the magic of Christmas.

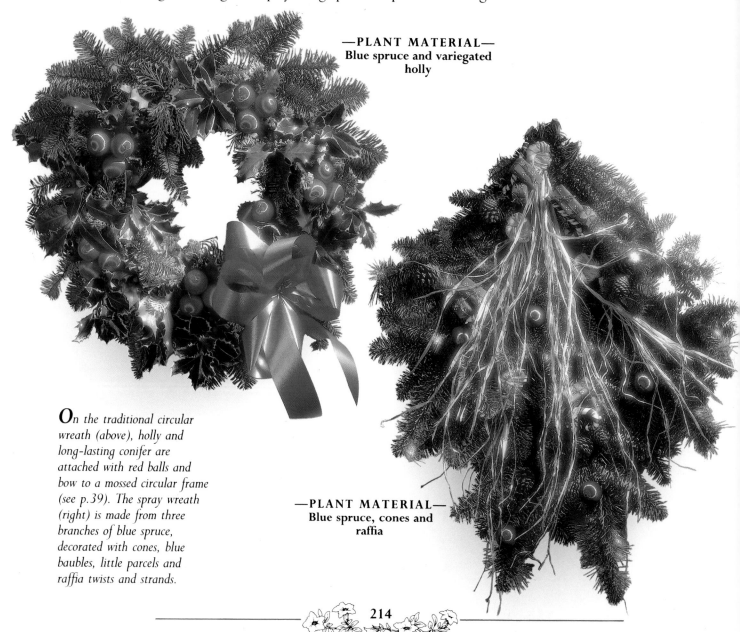

—PLANT MATERIAL—
Blue spruce and variegated holly

*O*n the traditional circular wreath (above), holly and long-lasting conifer are attached with red balls and bow to a mossed circular frame (see p.39). The spray wreath (right) is made from three branches of blue spruce, decorated with cones, blue baubles, little parcels and raffia twists and strands.

—PLANT MATERIAL—
Blue spruce, cones and raffia

*S*imply decorated with red
and green tartan ribbon bows
and small red, silver and green
parcels, this Christmas tree
makes an effective centrepiece.

—PLANT MATERIAL—
**Moss, blue spruce and
tangerines**

Robust garland

Chicken-wire stuffed with
moss (see p.211) forms the
basis of this swag. Push or
wire conifer sprigs into the
frame, then thread wired fruits
into the moss base. Add the
artificial cherries last.

Of the three different types of garlanding on these pages, the robust garland at far left would look best flat against a wall, maybe flagging a mirror or surrounding a window. The more delicate garland in the centre would be ideal for a shelf, mantelpiece or around a painting, and the traditional-looking swag at top left would look good adorning a large fireplace in a living room.

—PLANT MATERIAL—
Douglas fir and cones, holly and elaeagnus

Traditional garland

Lay out overlapping fir branches with cones, making the shape that you want to create. Tie the branches together in several places, making sure that they are held together securely.

Fill out the garland by tying in pieces of berried holly and elaeagnus along the whole length.

Delicate garland

Plait strands of raffia to the length you require the garland to be. Then thread groups of gold-sprayed butcher's-broom leaves and silver-sprayed larch cone twigs into the plait at regular intervals. For an even more festive look, add wired gold balls into each clump of plant material.

—PLANT MATERIAL—
Raffia, butcher's-broom and larch cone twigs

*T*erracotta saucers and pots here display an array of nuts and fruits that are so popular at Christmas time. The large saucer is filled with moss and a wet-foam-filled ball of chicken-wire placed on top. Box and holly sprigs are fixed into the foam, and wired lychees are added to complete the Christmas pudding topiary. Flowers could also be added if you wished. Nuts and fruit are displayed on the moss beneath. The arrangement will last over the whole of the Christmas period until twelfth night on 5th January.

—**PLANT MATERIAL**—
Moss, box, holly, lychees, pecans, walnuts, kumquats, hemlock, fir cones, dried mushrooms and tangerines

*T*he brilliant reds and greens of the roses, butcher's-broom and berries give this glowing dinner party centrepiece a really festive look. Green candles will enhance the Christmas mood.

—**PLANT MATERIAL**—
Red roses, rowan, snowberries and butcher's-broom

A grand epergne in three tiers cascades with violent red and bright pink flowers.

—**PLANT MATERIAL**—
Red roses, pink orchids, statice, broccoli, variegated holly, rush leaves, ivy, red tulips and grapes

Grand epergne

Attach prongs to the two glass bases and fix wet foam on to them. Wire a few large grape bunches around the centre column.

Secure the plant material in the foam. Then, using the same ingredients, create a fan-shaped arrangement in the vase on top.

Growing for arranging

Growing plants has to be one of the most magical and rewarding occupations in existence. To watch a plant as it develops individual characteristics and its first leaves take shape is breathtaking. Then, to gaze as it develops a definite form, growing into a mature specimen, is a truly wondrous experience. Of course, this is sometimes not possible: although many plants grow to maturity in a season, others take up to 100 years to develop. Plants vary so much in leaf shape and flower type that it is often difficult to see how they can be in any way related. For example, a fern frond and the huge leaves of *Gunnera mannicata*, which can span many feet, seem to belong to different planets.

Even in winter there is an exciting and extremely varied array of flowers, foliage and seed-heads, nearly all of which can be used in arrangements in any number of combinations. So there is never any chance of becoming bored with arranging fresh flowers, as you need never create the same arrangement twice.

Cottage gardens

Traditionally, the cottage garden was a practical sort of garden, one in which to grow vegetables and fruits, with a few flowers added haphazardly for some extra colour in the summer. There was usually a straight path from the garden gate to the front door, which was frequently edged with flowering plants such as lavender, rosemary and pinks. There would also be a flowerbed running right in front of the house, some climbing roses rambling over the walls and some towering holly-hocks standing sentinel between the windows.

Things have changed a bit during the last few years as more and more cottages have been bought by town folk for use as weekend getaways. Of course, there are still plenty of real cottage gardens, but there are also plenty of gardens that set out to capture the cottage garden mood, a romantic idea of the old, rambling cottage garden, which is somewhat removed from the original practical cottage garden.

The straight path now takes a deviating turn to the left and to the right before landing up at the front door, and the vegetables are relegated to a patch at the back where they are not on general view. Where the rows of vegetables used to be, today is a riot of colourful perennials and annuals, and it all looks very beautiful.

Cottage flowers are friendly, sunny, unsophisticated flowers. They come in all the colours of the rainbow and they smell as sweet as they look. As well as the traditional plants like lavender and rosemary, the tall and colourful hollyhocks, the lovely pinks and old-fashioned roses, there are all sorts of daisies, foxgloves and feverfew, love-lies-bleeding and larkspur. Other cottage plants include sweet rockets and sweet

sultans, Michaelmas daisies and campanulas, tall clumps of yarrow and patches of violets and pansies. There may also be some box or yew clipped neatly into a cone or a ball shape and set by the front door. More recently the fashion has been to include lots of silver foliage plants, like artemisia, santolina and helichrysum amongst the more traditional and well-loved cottage flowers. A mixed hedge of hawthorn, beech and wild roses makes an ideal boundary.

Introduce plants like buddleias that will attract plenty of butterflies; plant mullein to keep the moles at bay; and add plenty of herbs not too far from the kitchen — rosemary, sage and thyme are all attractive plants (left).

This pretty, informal lilac and pink mix (right) is a favourite of mine. The low basket is covered with sphagnum moss, tied on with lengths of raffia, for a very cottagey, natural look.

—PLANT MATERIAL—
Fleabane, pinks, pink yarrow, lilac bellflowers and potted freesias

The making of this sort of romantic cottage garden is not as simple as it may seem. To achieve a wonderful, seemingly higgledy-piggledy array of flowers and greenery, you must plan very carefully, especially if you want the garden to look attractive for more than just the summer months. You must create hills, valleys and plains filled with many different colours and forms. This is done by means of a strong structure of perennial plants and shrubs, leaving spaces between for groups of annuals to be grown.

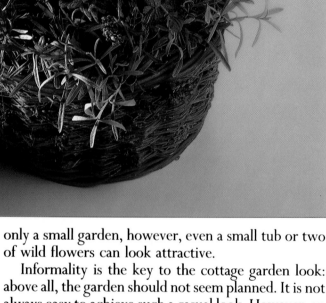

*L*avender is the epitome of cottage garden flowers (far right). Not only does it produce a mound of pretty flowers over a long period, but it also has a wonderful scent and lovely silvery foliage. There are several species of lavender and many varieties, giving a colour range from purple to white.

*T*he basket for this cottage arrangement (right) is made from dried lavender, which retains its scent for many months. The arrangement is very informal – the lavender looks as though it could be growing. The purple and pink bracts of clary last for a long time both on the plant and in arrangements. Here, a few sprigs are added to give some extra "cottage" interest.

—PLANT MATERIAL—
Lavender and clary

Because there is quite a lot of maintenance in the upkeep of a cottage garden, many people choose to have a stretch of lawn as well as some flowery beds. A lawn was not traditionally part of the cottage garden, though; all the space was given over to growing flowers and vegetables. Today, however, it would not look out of place, provided it was not kept quite as well as a cricket green, and you allowed the odd, stray clump of primroses, and patches of daisies and butter-cups to seed and grow there.

Sometimes, if an orchard made up some of the domain, you would find rough grass below the trees mixed with wild meadow flowers, all of which were cut a couple of times during the summer. Meadow seed mixes are now readily available and if you have the space there is nothing nicer than having a wild area in your cottage garden. You can mow a wiggly path through the meadow, leading to a spot under a tree where you can sit on the sunniest days. If you have only a small garden, however, even a small tub or two of wild flowers can look attractive.

Informality is the key to the cottage garden look: above all, the garden should not seem planned. It is not always easy to achieve such a casual look. However, an interesting patchwork of simple and colourful plants, both in their flowers and their foliage, will do much towards evoking this atmosphere.

Cottage garden arrangements

A cottage garden will supply you with material for a host of arrangements throughout the whole year. Cot-tage garden flowers, herbs and foliage make beautiful and colourful flower arrangements that look at their best in the simplest of containers, such as stone jugs and mugs or old baskets. The flowers in such arrange-ments should look as though they have just been picked and placed at random in the container, and should give the impression that they are still growing.

Country gardens

Anyone who owns a house with a country garden can count themselves lucky indeed. The essential country garden combines elements of the countryside with plantings of shrubs and flowers. Like the cottage garden, it is informal in style, but a country garden is very unlikely not to boast in addition lawns and borders, and trees and shrubs – all relating to the house around which they stand. There are no strict rules to adhere to when designing a country garden save that nature must be your guide.

The house should be the starting point for such a garden. Why not have a terrace that gives on to the house and that is reasonably close to the kitchen, so that on warm, summer evenings you can have dinner out in the garden? From the terrace, devise borders that lead the eye across the lawn either to the surrounding countryside or, if there are nearby buildings, to a natural barrier of trees or hedges. It is best not to be able to see all the garden at once and so, although lovely views are important, some sort of compartmentalization is a very good idea, providing the garden with a sense of mystery and excitement.

Colour can be carefully controlled or riotous, depending on your taste. Try to give different areas of the garden different characteristics. A border on the shadier side of the garden may well look best with pale-coloured or even all white flowers, whereas a sunny border can be full of bright cheerful colours. You can mix and combine colours or stick to simple colour schemes. Whatever colours you choose, the borders should have a good breadth and plants should be given plenty of room to attain their mature shapes without encroaching on each other.

Large-sized borders must have a good structure of shrubs and perennial plants, unless you have a great deal of time to devote to a herbaceous border. Such borders can look magnificent, but the plants need a large amount of staking and general management throughout the year to keep them looking at their best, and their flowering period is usually limited to about six weeks of the summer at most. Foliage can play an important role in the country garden. After all,

This sun-drenched herbaceous border backed by trees (left) contains clumps of phlox and campanulas, lilies and evening primroses, montbretia, heleniums and the great yellow broom, which drips its brilliant colour over everything. All these flowers, save the evening primroses, are good cut flowers and they make the sort of informal arrangements that suit country house interiors so well, linking and matching the outside to the inside.

A haze of summer flowers grows out of the green glass jug (right) that sits on a country kitchen window ledge, alongside an enchanting matching vase.

—PLANT MATERIAL—
Saponaria, yarrow, lady's mantle, feverfew, corn marigolds, hydrangea head, poppy, cornflowers, catmint and echium

green is the main colour that links the garden with the countryside around it. Hedges and topiary can produce a wide variety of different greens and, at the same time, help to create interest in the garden by dividing and screening its many areas.

China bowls and jugs, and glass and pewter vases are the most suitable containers for country arrangements. Keep together the flowers picked from specific borders, to make interesting groupings of forms and colours that reflect the border.

—**PLANT MATERIAL**—
**White tulips, artemisia,
skimmia and Mexican
orange foliage**

*A compartmentalized country
garden allows for some really
interesting juxtapositions of
plants, both in form and
colour. In this garden,
photographed in late spring,
there is a striking contrast
between the golden and silver
greens of the clipped box and
the dark yew hedges in the
background and the informal
planting of white tulips amid
silver artemisia foliage beneath
a silver-leaved weeping pear in
the foreground.*

*The same colours and forms
combine well in the gentle
country arrangement (above)
created in a simple, mid-
nineteenth-century jug.*

—————— *Wild & formal gardens* ——————

*I*t takes a great deal of contrivance to make a garden or section of a garden look acceptable yet wild. Perhaps "informal" is a more apt word than "wild". However they are described, such gardens are places where plants tumble over one another in an abandoned, wild-looking way, which is in fact achieved by careful design. They do not have to be filled with wild flowers, although there is little that is more beautiful than a meadow filled with grasses and wild flowers.

It is wonderful to have an area of the garden that is wild-looking: perhaps an orchard with long grass and well-spaced fruit trees, a place that attracts the birds, butterflies and bees; or an area of woodland with bluebells underneath the trees. For a garden with a stream, why not plant lots of the moisture-loving plants like primulas, ferns, marsh marigolds and bulrushes? For the plants to do their best, it is often prudent to tame the wilder elements. For instance, willows planted beside a stream will become very large quite quickly and the underplanting will soon suffer. To rectify this the willow trees should be pollarded, which will often create some really interesting shapes. When you plant a wild garden, don't despair if some plants don't survive. Wild flowers often have a delicacy that belies their true strength, but those that *do* survive you can be sure are strong.

In the wild or informal garden there are no hard edges, but in the formal garden there are strong straight lines and strong curves, squares, rectangles and circles. The idea of the formal garden is centuries old. In it nature conforms to the rules of shape and proportion. In seventeenth-century gardens order

ruled and there was little of the countryside to be reflected within their confines. Plants were clipped and shaped severely. However, plants have a knack of looking slightly disordered and, even within the formal structures, the planting of herbs and lilies had a way of looking relaxed and at home, partially breaking the formal lines of the garden.

A formal structure softened by a mixture of formal and informal plantings is one that I particularly love in

*S*o that the underplanting does not suffer, willows planted beside a stream should be pollarded as here, creating an unusual, striking border. Ferns, hellebores and spring bulbs thrive amongst the rocks beside a stream, creating an idyllic-looking scene. In winter, the rather stark border looks even more dramatic.

*T*his informal bunch of Lenten roses has a slightly Japanese feel to it. The deep plum-coloured jug enhances the colours of the flowers perfectly. To make the roses last, they must be pricked a few times down their stems before being arranged in a vase of warm water.

—**PLANT MATERIAL**—
Lenten roses

a garden. Such a combination easily translates to flower arrangements too. For instance, those grander, more formal arrangements – the pedestal and fireplace creations – with their strong, bony structures are softened by the irregular curves and shapes of the flowers and foliage, whilst retaining their formal, symmetrical shape at the same time. The natural informality of flowers will always remove any rigidity from a formal shape, whether a border in the garden or an elaborate arrangement in a vase indoors.

This formal topiary tree looks simple yet effective. To make it, spike a wet foam ball on to a piece of branch set into plaster-of-Paris in a pot. Then arrange flowers and foliage in the ball to form a tree shape and surround the base of the branch with moss.

—PLANT MATERIAL—
Golden yew and dill

In this garden, formality and informality go hand in hand. The hedges, the path and the clipped box balls and spirals are all very formal and restrained, but the plants in between clothe the bones prettily, sneaking out of line occasionally. Topiary means that plants can be used architecturally to form bold shapes, which help define the structure of a garden.

Spring & summer gardens

Out of the blue, or more likely out of the grey, on a dreary mid-winter's day suddenly you sense that spring is just around the corner. I am never quite sure what it is that brings about this feeling; perhaps it is something to do with the change in atmospheric pressure, or maybe a sound or smell triggers off the thought. Whatever the reason, from then on winter is much easier to cope with and surprisingly soon the first real signs of spring are upon us.

Spring seems a particularly yellow time of the year for flowers. This is so, in spite of the fact that spring flowers are many coloured with some good blues in hyacinths, scillas, grape hyacinths and bluebells, which echo the colour of the spring skies. Somehow it is the yellows that sing out from the newly awakening earth. There are the daffodils that stand so upright in great patches of brilliant colour, and the smaller flower-heads of primroses, growing on grassy banks and at the bottom of hedgerows. In the spring gardens there are great bushes of forsythia as well as the daffodils and all the other types of narcissus: jonquils and soleil d'or with their intoxicating scents, the smaller daffodil 'Peeping Tom' and the double-flowered 'Golden Ducat'.

Of course, there are white-flowered narcissus as well. 'Actaea' has ice-white petals with a small bright orange corona at its centre; 'Rippling Waters' is all white, and some newer varieties have peachy-pink coronas and white, cream or yellow petals. Nearly all the narcissus are scented and some, like 'Trevithian', have an overpowering fragrance. Green is the other spring colour. First it is seen mostly at ground level as the grass takes on a new lease of life, then slowly it gains height as the first willows and then the early chestnuts take on a green, leafy haze.

By this time the sun has a new warmth and it is good to be out of doors. At this point the colour range of flowers begins to expand, for summer has begun. The wonderful sweet-scented irises (commonly known as flags) are flowering, and the sunshine is drawing out the last perfume of the wallflowers. Late tulips open so wide that they appear to be gasping for air and the first rose buds begin to show their colours. Fresh green is everywhere and in the mornings the garden hums with the excitement of approaching summer.

The summer garden is a rich and bountiful place with an array of wonderful flowers to arrange. There are enormous paeonies in pinks and reds, and creams and white. Picked as the buds begin to open, they last for nearly a week and then leave a beautiful scattering of petals. They mix well with mock orange, with its fragrant white flowers, and with spires of stocks.

This romantic view in early spring (left) depicts daffodils surrounding a boathouse across a stretch of still water. The banks are moss-covered and there is a haze of new green appearing on the trees. In the air, too, there is the first promise of the better weather to come in summer.

Daffodils have a great natural strength, both in form and colour, and they look at their best in a natural-looking container, like the moss-covered basket (right). They will last extremely well once cut if they are placed outside. Otherwise, picked in bud, they will open quite quickly indoors, where they will still last several days in peak flowering form.

—PLANT MATERIAL—
Daffodils and carpet moss

—PLANT MATERIAL—
Irises and tulips

*M*onet's garden (right) is an exciting vision of colour, and is the subject of many of his Impressionist paintings. Here, just on the edge of summer, the irises are poised and cool in their pastel colours amongst the more flamboyant-looking wallflowers and tulips.

A tall, cylindrical container with a matt, purplish-blue glaze (above) bursts open with white, yellow and blue irises and pink tulips, echoing the mood of Monet's shimmering, colourful garden.

There are thousands of varieties of rose. My favourites are the old-fashioned ones that open flat and quartered and have a rich, fruity scent, such as 'Mme Hardy', 'Mme Pierre Oger', 'Charles de Mills' and 'Variegata di Bologna'. Once cut, they are not as long-lasting as the Hybrid Tea roses, but their beauty far surpasses the more modern roses. No, this is not quite true, for there are many new varieties that have a similar shape and scent to the old roses but, unlike their ancestors, are perpetual or at least have a good repeat flowering. Around the base of the roses – for they are not very beautifully shaped shrubs – it is a good idea to grow some plants that have attractive foliage as well as flowers: lavenders, santolinas, artemisia and lady's mantle all mix well with roses.

Colour follows colour in a wonderful long succession of summer flowers. The brilliant blue of delphiniums, which stand so tall; the pink, white and blue of larkspur; the yellow of yarrow; the sunny mixes of geraniums and annuals like godetias; the rich-coloured panicles of the strangely scented phlox; the pinks and the carnations of all colours, many with spicy clove scents; and the cornflowers as blue as the sky should be at this wonderful time of the year. Summer is the time when plants put on their greatest show and arrangements can look simply wonderful. With the rich abundance of flowers that are available, you can be really creative and experiment with using different mixes and combinations of flowers in your arrangements. In fact, there is no need to repeat the same arrangement twice in summer.

Collecting flowers from the garden is that much easier with a trug. Lay out the flowers thoughtfully, to give an idea of how they will look once they are arranged.

—PLANT MATERIAL—
Stocks, cow parsley, love-in-a-mist, decorative onions, hebe and bellflowers

Plant guide

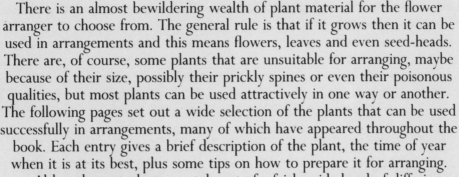

There is an almost bewildering wealth of plant material for the flower
arranger to choose from. The general rule is that if it grows then it can be
used in arrangements and this means flowers, leaves and even seed-heads.
There are, of course, some plants that are unsuitable for arranging, maybe
because of their size, possibly their prickly spines or even their poisonous
qualities, but most plants can be used attractively in one way or another.
The following pages set out a wide selection of the plants that can be used
successfully in arrangements, many of which have appeared throughout the
book. Each entry gives a brief description of the plant, the time of year
when it is at its best, plus some tips on how to prepare it for arranging.
    Although most plants are tolerant of a fairly wide band of differing
planting conditions, some need the soil to be acid or alkaline rather than
neutral, whilst others will not tolerate too much cold or indeed too much
heat. In this plant guide, the plants' specific likes and dislikes are
highlighted to help you choose plants that will be suitable for the soil and
climate that you can provide. It is always well worth the trouble of finding
out in advance whether the plants you wish to grow will thrive.

Preparing flowers before arranging

Whether you grow your own flowers or buy them from a flower shop, all
plant material must be prepared before arranging. The stems must be cut
at a sharp angle with a pair of good kitchen or florists' scissors, and any
leaves that might go under the water level must be removed, before giving
the plant a good drink of water. Some plants then need further treatment:
woody stems need crushing, stems containing milky sap need singeing to
seal them, while some flowers and foliage like to be started off in near-
boiling water to encourage them to take water up their stems. The
requirements of each plant are specified in the plant guide.
    Each of the seasons of the year gives us a different selection of plant
material. Summer is the time when there are more flowers available than at
any other time of the year, winter the least. Spring is a particularly yellow
time, whereas autumn has a predominance of oranges and rusts. There is
certainly a great deal of overlap between the seasons and many plants will
flower maybe late in one season as well as early in the next. Frequently,
too, the seasons themselves vary and a mild winter may produce spring
flowers as much as a month earlier than usual.

It is always difficult to say which plants are the most beautiful. Each one
has its own special attributes that can look attractive in association with
others. The secret of creating a beautiful flower arrangement is really a
question of finding shapes and colours that look interesting with each
other. But the main thing to remember when arranging flowers is that it
should be great fun to do. Everything about plants is beautiful and it is a
joy to choose a selection and put them together in your own creation.

Acacia **Mimosa, wattle**
Trees with clusters of fragrant yellow flowers and grey-green, finely cut leaves.
MEANING Secret love, friendship.
AVAILABILITY Spring.
PLANTING CONDITIONS Must be considered conservatory or greenhouse plants except in frost-free areas. Silver wattle takes a little frost.
CONDITIONING Hammer the stems, place in deep water and cover with plastic bag for a day.

Acanthus **Bear's breeches**
Herbaceous plants with tall spikes of mauve, purple/white hooded flowers, with large, handsome glossy leaves. Long lasting in water.
MEANING Fine arts, artifice.
AVAILABILITY Late summer. Can be used dried.
PLANTING CONDITIONS Well-drained soil. Sunny position, but will tolerate some shade.
CONDITIONING Dip stems in boiling water and stand in deep water for three to four hours.

Acer **Maple**
Trees with green, yellow, brown, purple foliage, plus good autumn tints. Some maples are very slow growing and therefore unsuitable for repeated cutting. Some have excellent young foliage and fragrant flowers in spring.
MEANING Reserve.
AVAILABILITY Summer for natural leaf colours; autumn for tints.
PLANTING CONDITIONS Any soil, in sun or partial shade.
CONDITIONING Hammer the stems and place in deep water for several hours. Float or submerge individual leaves for small arrangements.

Achillea **Yarrow**
Large, flat-headed, yellow flowers over a feathery foliage. Also pink/red and white varieties. *A. ptarmica* has white button-like flowers. All long lasting.
MEANING War.
AVAILABILITY Summer and autumn. Can be used dried.
PLANTING CONDITIONS Good soil, sun.
CONDITIONING Crush stems and leave in deep water.

Acidanthera
White gladiolus-type flowers with dark blotches in the throat. Sweetly scented. Tall with thin long leaves.
AVAILABILITY Early autumn.
PLANTING CONDITIONS Sunny borders in spring. Lift and store after flowering.
CONDITIONING Stand in deep water for several hours.

Aconitum **Monkshood**
Tall spikes of deep blue, hooded flowers. Also lighter blue, white and cream varieties. Poisonous.
MEANING Misanthropy.
AVAILABILITY Summer and autumn. Can be used dried.
PLANTING CONDITIONS Any soil; sun or shade.

CONDITIONING Stand in deep water for several hours.

Aesculus **Horse chestnut**
Trees with "sticky buds" opening in water to reveal young leaves. Brown shiny fruit or "conkers". The huge leaves look good with clusters of the maturing fruit in large arrangements.
MEANING Luxury.
AVAILABILITY Buds in spring; fruit in autumn.
PLANTING CONDITIONS Any soil; sun or light shade.
CONDITIONING Hammer stems and stand them in deep water.

Agapanthus **African lily**
Round globes of blue flowers in various shades. Also white varieties. Strap-like leaves. Last quite well in water.
AVAILABILITY Late summer to autumn.
PLANTING CONDITIONS Good soil, preferably moist. Full sun. Not all varieties are hardy.
CONDITIONING Stand in deep water for several hours.

Ajuga **Bugle**
Short ground-covering plants with spikes of blue flowers. There are varieties with pink flowers and also those with variegated or coloured leaves. Medium lasting. Pretty in miniature arrangements.
AVAILABILITY Spring and summer.
PLANTING CONDITIONS Cool, shady conditions. Any soil.
CONDITIONING Stand in deep water for several hours.

Alchemilla **Lady's mantle**
Feathery sprays of small, green-yellow flowers. Soft, round leaves holding pearls of water. Long lasting.
AVAILABILITY Spring to early autumn. Can also be dried.
PLANTING CONDITIONS Any soil. Sun or shade. Self-seeding.
CONDITIONING Stand in deep water for several hours.

Allium **Decorative onion**
Bulbs producing round globes of purple or pink flowers. Also blue, white and yellow varieties. Long lasting.
AVAILABILITY Spring and summer. Can also be used dried.
PLANTING CONDITIONS Well-drained soil. Full sun.
CONDITIONING Stand in deep water before arranging.

Alstroemeria **Peruvian lily**
Trumpets of pink, red, orange, yellow and white on longish stems. Good seed pods. Medium lasting.
AVAILABILITY Summer in gardens. All year from florists.
PLANTING CONDITIONS Any soil. Full sun. Some are not frost-hardy.
CONDITIONING Stand in deep water for several hours.

Althaea **Hollyhock**
Old-fashioned flowers with very tall

spikes of red, pink, purple, yellow, or white. Good seed-heads.
MEANING Ambition, fruitfulness, fecundity.
AVAILABILITY Summer.
PLANTING CONDITIONS Any soil. Sunny position.
CONDITIONING Boil stems and stand in deep water for several hours before using.

Amaranthus **Love-lies-bleeding**
Half-hardy annual plants with long ropes of crimson flowers. Also green variety available. Long lasting.
MEANING Hopeless, not heartless.
AVAILABILITY Summer and autumn. Can also be used dried.
PLANTING CONDITIONS Well-drained, rich soil. Full sun. Sow annually.
CONDITIONING Remove most of the leaves and stand in deep water for several hours.

Amaryllis **Belladonna lily**
Bulbs with fragrant pink or white flowers on long stems. Can be used as pot plants.
MEANING Pride, haughtiness, silence.
AVAILABILITY Autumn in gardens. Winter and spring from florists.
PLANTING CONDITIONS Any soil. Full sun. Slightly tender.
CONDITIONING Stand in deep water for several hours.
SEE ALSO *Hippeastrum,* **Amaryllis**

Ananas **Pineapple**
The fruit of the common pineapple.
MEANING You are perfect.
AVAILABILITY Summer and autumn.
PLANTING CONDITIONS Can be grown in a hot house.

Anaphalis **Pearl everlasting**
Silver-grey foliage plants with small white, yellow-centred flowers.
AVAILABILITY Summer and autumn. Can be used dried.
PLANTING CONDITIONS Any soil that is not too dry. Full sun or sunny with a little shade.
CONDITIONING Stand in deep water for several hours before using.

Anemone **Windflower**
There are several distinct anemones. First there are the spring-flowering types: wood anemones which are short and delicate in shades of white, pink and blue; and the De Caen types which are bright and in brash shades of red, blue and mauve. The autumn-flowering Japanese anemones are much taller and robust. These are white or pink.
MEANING Forlornness, forsaken, sickness.
AVAILABILITY Spring or autumn. De Caen are available from florists for most of the year.
PLANTING CONDITIONS Wood anemones need cool, shady conditions; De Caen anemones need full sun; Japanese anemones will tolerate either.
CONDITIONING Stand in deep water for several hours.

Angelica
Large, white-green domes of flowers and bold foliage. Tall. Usually found in the herb garden. Both flowers and seed-heads good in arrangements.
MEANING Soaring thoughts.
AVAILABILITY Summer. Dried: all year.
PLANTING CONDITIONS Sun or light shade. Prefers moist soil.
CONDITIONING Dip in boiling water and then stand in deep water for several hours.

Anthriscus **Cow parsley, queen Anne's lace**
Tall, wild plants of the hedgerows with large, flat heads of white flowers above delicate, lacy foliage. Last well but tend to exude a fine, sticky honeydew over everything.
AVAILABILITY Spring.
PLANTING CONDITIONS Sun or light shade, preferably in the wild garden.
CONDITIONING Boil stems then stand in deep water for several hours.

Anthurium **Painter's palette**
Greenhouse plants with heart-shaped leaves and a curious cylindrical flower coming from a bright-coloured, heart-shaped bract. Exotic looking. Five hundred species giving a large variety of colour and shape. Very long lasting in water.
AVAILABILITY Summer. All year from florists.
PLANTING CONDITIONS Pot plant in warm moist atmosphere in greenhouse or conservatory.
CONDITIONING Stand in deep water for several hours.

Antirrhinum **Snapdragon**
Annual bedding plants. Old-fashioned looking flowers with a good range of all colours except blue. The modern varieties, particularly the F1 hybrids, are the best for arrangements. Short lasting in water.
MEANING Presumption.
AVAILABILITY Summer.
PLANTING CONDITIONS Any good soil in full sun.
CONDITIONING Stand in deep water for several hours.

Aquilegia **Columbine, granny's bonnet**
Old-fashioned cottage flowers. Short-lived in water but good as cut flowers because of the shape and variety of colours. All are suitable for cutting but McKana hybrids are the best.
MEANING Folly. Red: anxious and trembling. Purple: resolution.
AVAILABILITY Summer.
PLANTING CONDITIONS Good soil in sun or light shade.
CONDITIONING Stand in deep water for several hours.

Arbutus **Strawberry tree**
Unusual trees in that the white flowers and the previous year's berries appear at the same time. The fruit look like strawberries.
MEANING Esteem and love.

AVAILABILITY Late autumn.
PLANTING CONDITIONS Any soil, prefer light shade. Very slow growing.
CONDITIONING Crush stems. Stand in deep water for several hours.

Armeria Thrift, sea pink
Cushions with short stems topped by a pink head of flowers. Deep pink and red varieties available. Leaves of no significance in arrangements. Quite a long life in water.
MEANING Sympathy.
AVAILABILITY Summer. Can also be used dried.
PLANTING CONDITIONS Any soil, full sun.
CONDITIONING Stand in deep water for short while.

Artemisia Wormwood
Valuable for their tall stems of silvery-grey foliage. Flowers insignificant except for *A. lactiflora* which has green leaves and masses of small cream flowers. Long lasting in water.
MEANING Absence.
AVAILABILITY Summer and autumn.
PLANTING CONDITIONS Any well-drained soil. Full sun.
CONDITIONING Crush woody stems, boil ends and then stand in deep water for several hours.

Arum Cuckoo-pint, lords-and-ladies
Native plants useful for their shiny spring foliage. *A. italicum* 'Pictum' is valuable as it has leaves with cream marbling throughout the winter. The spikes of red berries are also useful.
MEANING Ardour.
AVAILABILITY Leaves: winter and spring. Berries: autumn.
PLANTING CONDITIONS Moist woodland conditions.
CONDITIONING Submerge leaves in water for several hours.
SEE ALSO *Zantedeschia*, **Arum lily**

Arundinaria Bamboo
Slender stems with grass-like leaves. Rarely flowers.
AVAILABILITY All year. Can be used dried.
PLANTING CONDITIONS Any soil, sun or light shade.
CONDITIONING Two or three minutes in boiling vinegar to prevent leaves curling, then stand in deep water for several hours.

Asparagus
Valuable for the spikes or spears when they first appear, or tall fine, feathery foliage later on. In autumn they carry red berries, but the leaves drop readily once they start yellowing.
AVAILABILITY Spears: early summer. Foliage: summer.
PLANTING CONDITIONS Well-drained soil in full sun.
CONDITIONING Stand in deep water for several hours.

Aster Michaelmas daisy
A good range of tall, brightly coloured daisies. There are many cultivars available and also quite a number of more delicate species with airy sprays of small flowers. They last very well in water.
MEANING Afterthought.
AVAILABILITY Autumn.
PLANTING CONDITIONS Any soil in full sun. Do not overcrowd.
CONDITIONING Crush woody stems, dip in boiling water and then stand in deep water for several hours.
SEE ALSO *Callistephus*, **China aster**

Astilbe
Tapering plumes of feathery flowers in a range of colours from pink through mauves to red as well as white and cream. Lots of varieties to choose from. The leaves are also very decorative. Not long lasting in water. Worth cutting after brown seed-heads have formed.
AVAILABILITY Summer. Seed-heads: autumn.
PLANTING CONDITIONS Moist soil. Partial shade or sun.
CONDITIONING Stand in deep water for several hours.

Astrantia Masterwort
Curiously shaped greenish-white flowers, each like a little posy. There are shell pink and red forms. Medium height with good foliage. Last well in water. Combine well with phlox and larkspur.
AVAILABILITY Summer and autumn.
PLANTING CONDITIONS Any soil in sun or partial shade.
CONDITIONING Stand in deep water for several hours.

Aucuba Spotted laurel
Shrubs useful for their all-year-round shiny green foliage. There are also variegated forms. Female plants also carry brilliant red berries.
MEANING Perfidy.
AVAILABILITY All year. Berries: autumn and winter.
PLANTING CONDITIONS Any soil, sun or light shade.
CONDITIONING Crush woody stems, then stand in deep water for several hours.

Azalea
A type of *Rhododendron* with brightly coloured flowers. They can be used as cut flowers or dwarf varieties can be grown in pots for display. Many cultivars are available; some are particularly fragrant. Do not last long in water.
MEANING Temperance.
AVAILABILITY Spring, winter in pots if forced.
PLANTING CONDITIONS Lime-free soil, light shade. Pots: soil-less compost.
CONDITIONING Hammer woody stems and place in warm water; allow to cool for several hours.

Ballota
Perennials or sub-shrubs valuable for their furry, circular leaves, which are cupped around the arching stems. The hairs give the leaves a greyish-green appearance. The flowers are insignificant. Last very well in water.
AVAILABILITY Summer and autumn.
PLANTING CONDITIONS Any soil. Full sun.
CONDITIONING Put stem ends in boiling water for a few minutes, then stand in deep water, not submerging the leaves.

Banksia
Australian evergreen trees and shrubs with dramatic cones of yellow or red flowers. Tender and can only be grown in conservatories or greenhouses except in very mild areas.
AVAILABILITY Summer.
PLANTING CONDITIONS Moist soil in full sun.
CONDITIONING Crush woody stems then stand in deep water for several hours.

Begonia
Bright, colourful pot plants with green, ear-shaped leaves. Some forms are large and blousey. There are white, yellow, and pink through to red cultivars. Some such as *B. rex* are grown for their foliage. Many varieties available. Tender so should be over-wintered inside.
AVAILABILITY All year indoors.
PLANTING CONDITIONS Soil-less potting compost.

Berberis Barberry
Spiny shrubs with green or purple foliage and yellow or orange flowers. Red berries are particularly useful in autumn.
MEANING Sourness, sharpness, bad-temper.
AVAILABILITY Foliage: spring to autumn, some species all year. Flowers: spring. Berries: autumn.
PLANTING CONDITIONS Any soil. Sun or partial shade.
CONDITIONING Crush woody stems and then stand in deep water for several hours.

Bergenia Elephant ear
Large fleshy-leaved plants with drooping spikes of varying shades of pink flowers. Both leaves and flowers good for arrangements.
AVAILABILITY Late winter, spring.
PLANTING CONDITIONS Any soil, sun or shade.
CONDITIONING Stand in deep water for several hours.

Betula Birch
These trees produce graceful bare branches in winter or sprays of fresh green leaves in spring. They also have small catkins in spring and catkin-like seed in autumn. The latter drop badly. There are many forms of birch with varying bark colour and leaf size.
MEANING Grace, meekness.
AVAILABILITY Branches: all year. Leaves: spring, summer.
PLANTING CONDITIONS Any soil. Sun or light shade.
CONDITIONING Hammer woody stems, then stand in deep water for several hours.

Bouvardia
Tender shrubs with tight heads of tubular flowers in pink, white and yellow. Some species are fragrant.
AVAILABILITY Late autumn, winter.
PLANTING CONDITIONS Greenhouse or conservatory.
CONDITIONING Crush woody stems, dip in boiling water and then stand in deep water for several hours.

Brassica Cabbage
Out of the context of the vegetable garden many brassicas are very decorative, not only the round leafy varieties, but the tall spires of Brussels sprouts, white and purple buds of broccolis, the white curds of cauliflowers and the curly leaves of kale. Both cabbages and Brussels have red forms. There are also brightly col-oured ornamental cabbages.
MEANING Gain, profit.
AVAILABILITY Cabbages: all year. Brussels, autumn and winter. Orna-mentals: autumn.
PLANTING CONDITIONS Any soil. Full sun.

Briza Quaking grass
Graceful grasses with drooping com-pact heads which move in the slightest draught. Pale green when fresh. Quite unlike any other grass in shape. Long lasting and can be used dried.
MEANING Agitation.
AVAILABILITY Summer and autumn. Can also be used dried.
PLANTING CONDITIONS Any soil. Sun.
CONDITIONING None.

Brodiaea
Bulbous plants similar to the decora-tive allium. Blue or purple heads on medium length stems. Leaves have often shrivelled before flower opens, so of no consequence.
AVAILABILITY Summer.
PLANTING CONDITIONS Greenhouse or warm spot outside. Any soil. Full sun.
CONDITIONING Stand in deep water for several hours.

Brunnera
These herbaceous plants have a myriad pale blue flowers floating above the heart-shaped leaves. Not very tall. Last reasonably well in water.
AVAILABILITY Early summer.
PLANTING CONDITIONS Moisture-reten-tive soil. Light shade.
CONDITIONING Boil stem ends, then stand in deep water for several hours.

Buddleia Butterfly bush
Fragrant shrubs with long spikes of mauve or purple flowers. Also species with globes of orange or yellow flowers. The foliage is either grey-silver or green. Do not last well.
AVAILABILITY Summer and autumn.
PLANTING CONDITIONS Any soil. Full sun.
CONDITIONING Dip stem ends in boiling water, then stand in deep water for several hours.

Buxus Box
Evergreen shrubs with small glossy

leaves. Last a very long time in water. Also variegated variety available. Very slow growing. Flowers of no consequence. Some might like the smell of the bruised leaves.
MEANING Stoicism.
AVAILABILITY All year.
PLANTING CONDITIONS Any soil. Full sun or light shade.
CONDITIONING Crush woody stems.

Caladium **Angel wings**
Tender pot plants grown for their foliage. The large, heart-shaped leaves have veins of a contrasting colour. The leaves can be green, white, cream or pale pink. They do not last long if cut.
AVAILABILITY Summer.
PLANTING CONDITIONS Moist, such as atmosphere in greenhouse or conservatory.
CONDITIONING If cut, submerge leaves in water for several hours before using in arrangements.

Calendula **Pot marigold**
Hardy annuals with bright yellow or orange flowers. Old-fashioned, cottage flowers. Will self-sow but resulting plants not so good as named cultivars. They last quite well in water.
MEANING Despair, grief, pain.
AVAILABILITY Summer.
PLANTING CONDITIONS Any well-drained soil. Full sun.
CONDITIONING Stand in deep water for several hours.

Callistemon **Bottle-brush tree**
Half-hardy and tender trees from Australia with beautiful bright red or yellow flowers with spikes of stamens that closely resemble bottle brushes.
AVAILABILITY Autumn. Can also be used dried.
PLANTING CONDITIONS Conservatory or warm greenhouse.
CONDITIONING Crush woody stems, then stand in deep water for several hours.

Callistephus **China aster**
Daisy-like annuals with a wide range of bright colours. Come in singles or doubles. Last well in water.
MEANING Variety.
AVAILABILITY Autumn.
PLANTING CONDITIONS Any soil. Sun.
CONDITIONING Stand in deep water for several hours.

Camassia **Quamash**
Bulbs producing long stems with spikes of large, star-shaped flowers in blue or white. They do not last very long in water but are valuable for their blue colour.
AVAILABILITY Summer.
PLANTING CONDITIONS Any fertile soil. Sun or light shade.
CONDITIONING Stand in deep water for several hours.

Camellia
Superb white, pink or red flowers set against glossy green leaves. Many

hardy cultivars to choose from. Long lasting in water.
MEANING White: loveliness. Red: excellence.
AVAILABILITY Late winter and spring. Earlier from florists.
PLANTING CONDITIONS Neutral or acid moisture-retentive soil. Dappled shade or sun but avoid early morning sun and cold winds.
CONDITIONING Hammer woody stems and then stand in deep water for several hours.

Campanula **Bellflower**
A vast range of blue flowers from very short to tall, the shorter having single bells, the taller whole spikes of flowers. Very cool in appearance. White forms are also available. They last well in water.
MEANING Tall: constancy. White: gratitude.
AVAILABILITY Summer.
PLANTING CONDITIONS Any well-drained soil. Full sun.
CONDITIONING Stand in deep water for several hours. Last longer if bees excluded from room.

Capsicum **Chillies, sweet pepper**
Green or bright red fruit with shiny skins producing good highlights in arrangements. Purchased fruit do not last as long as home-produced.
AVAILABILITY Autumn or all year from greengrocers.
PLANTING CONDITIONS Will grow outside but best in pots in a greenhouse. Keep moist.
CONDITIONING Polish.

Castanea **Sweet chestnut**
Multipurpose trees. Good, large-leaved foliage; fluffy yellow flowers (some might not like the smell) and finally light green, spiny fruit cases and shiny brown nuts.
MEANING Do me justice.
AVAILABILITY Leaves: spring, summer. Flowers: summer. Fruit cases and nuts: autumn.
PLANTING CONDITIONS Any soil. Full sun.
CONDITIONING Hammer stems and then stand in deep water for several hours. Polish nuts.

Catananche **Cupid's dart**
Pale blue, dark-eyed flowers with a papery calyx on thin stems. Very long lasting in water or as dried flowers.
MEANING Love approaches.
AVAILABILITY Summer and autumn. Also used dried.
PLANTING CONDITIONS Any well-drained soil. Full sun.
CONDITIONING Stand in deep water for several hours.

Cattleya
A wonderful range of epiphytic orchids with broad lips. The largest flowers can be up to 25cm (10in) across. Many species and cultivars are available giving a good range of colours with purple predominating. Some are fragrant. Short-stemmed and delicate.

AVAILABILITY All year.
PLANTING CONDITIONS Warm greenhouse.

Ceanothus **Californian lilac**
Evergreen and deciduous shrubs with fluffy round clusters of varying shades of blue flowers. The evergreen varieties have particularly good foliage.
AVAILABILITY Summer and early autumn.
PLANTING CONDITIONS Any soil. Can be tender so prefer sheltered position against a wall. Full sun.
CONDITIONING Hammer woody stems and then stand in deep water for several hours.

Celosia **Cock's comb**
Spectacular plants with bright red or yellow feathery plumes or crests.
MEANING Foppery, affectation.
AVAILABILITY Late summer and autumn.
PLANTING CONDITIONS Need greenhouse heat for best growth, but can be grown outside in sunny spot. Keep moist.
CONDITIONING Dip stem ends in boiling water, then stand in deep water for several hours.

Centaurea **Cornflower, sweet sultan**
Long lasting annuals. The basic colour is blue but there is now a good range including white, pink, mauve and red. Sweet sultan (*C. moschata*) is fragrant.
MEANING Delicacy.
AVAILABILITY Summer.
PLANTING CONDITIONS Any good soil. Full sun.
CONDITIONING Stand in deep water for several hours.

Centranthus **Valerian**
Large heads of deep pink or red flowers with fleshy stems and foliage. There are also white forms available.
MEANING Accommodating disposition.
AVAILABILITY Summer.
PLANTING CONDITIONS Any well-drained soil including poor soil. Sun.
CONDITIONING Stand in deep water for several hours.

Chaenomeles **Ornamental quince**
Waxy, apple-blossom type flowers clustered tight to the leafless branches. Mainly beautiful shades of red but also white, pink and orange. Curiously coloured, pear-shaped fruit.
AVAILABILITY Flowers: spring. Fruit: autumn.
PLANTING CONDITIONS Any good soil. Prefer support of a wall. Sun or shade.
CONDITIONING Hammer woody stems and then stand in deep water for several hours.

Chamaerops **Dwarf fan palm**
Trunkless palm trees. Leaves fan-like with 12–15 blades. The leaf stalks are spiny. Last very well when cut.
AVAILABILITY All year.
PLANTING CONDITIONS Greenhouse or conservatory except in very mild areas.

Cheiranthus **Wallflower**
The well-known wallflowers come in a

wide range of colours except blue. They are fragrant and last very well in water.
MEANING Fidelity in adversity or misfortune.
AVAILABILITY Spring.
PLANTING CONDITIONS Any soil. Full sun. Strictly they are perennials but best treated as biennials, discarding plants after flowering.
CONDITIONING Crush woody stems and then stand in deep water for several hours.

Chionodoxa **Glory of the snow**
Short-stemmed bulbs with delightful starry flowers, blue with a white throat. Pink forms are also available.
AVAILABILITY Spring.
PLANTING CONDITIONS Any good soil. Full sun.
CONDITIONING Stand in deep water for several hours.

Choisya **Mexican orange**
Clusters of white flowers surrounded by glossy leaves forming a natural posy. Very fragrant. Foliage valuable in its own right.
AVAILABILITY Flowers: summer. Foliage: all year.
PLANTING CONDITIONS Any free-draining soil. Sun preferred.
CONDITIONING Crush woody stems and then stand in deep water for several hours.

Chrysanthemum
One of the most popular cut flowers with their large range of shapes and warm colours. They last a very long time in water. Some people do not like the smell of the bruised foliage. Also available as pot plants.
MEANING Chinese: cheerfulness under adversity. Red: I love you. White: truth. Yellow: slighted love.
AVAILABILITY Autumn. All year from florists.
PLANTING CONDITIONS Good soil. Full sun.
CONDITIONING Crush woody stems, and then stand in deep water for several hours.

Cichorium **Endive**
Salad plants resembling lettuce with curly green or dissected leaves which are blanched before eating. Pretty blue flowers.
MEANING Frugality.
AVAILABILITY Autumn and early winter.
PLANTING CONDITIONS Light, well-drained soil. Full sun.

Cimifuga **Bugbane**
Long heads, almost like extended bottle brushes, with white or cream flowers. The long stems are a rich dark brown. Some have ferny leaves. Last reasonably well in water.
AVAILABILITY Summer and autumn.
PLANTING CONDITIONS Moisture-retentive soil. Cool position in light shade.
CONDITIONING Boil stem ends, then stand in deep water for several hours before using.

Clarkia Godetia
Easy-to-grow annuals with brightly col-oured flowers like funnels of crepe paper in pink, red, purple, orange and white. Some of the flowers are semi-double or double. Good by them-selves. Leaves insignificant. Last well in water.
AVAILABILITY Late spring, summer and autumn.
PLANTING CONDITIONS Any soil. Full sun.
CONDITIONING Dip stem ends in boiling water, then stand in deep water for several hours.

Clematis
Climbing and herbaceous plants. The smaller varieties make ideal trailing displays while the larger flowered can be used singly. The herbaceous varieties last better in water. Seed-heads are also valuable in arrangements.
MEANING Mental beauty. Evergreen: poverty.
AVAILABILITY Spring, summer and autumn. Seed-heeds: autumn.
PLANTING CONDITIONS Any rich soil; any situation as long as roots kept cool.
CONDITIONING Crush woody stems, dip stem ends in boiling water, and then stand in deep water for several hours.

Clivia Kaffir lily
Round heads of trumpet-shaped flowers in red and orange. Strap-shaped, glossy, dark green leaves. Last well in water. Pot plant.
AVAILABILITY Spring.
PLANTING CONDITIONS Warm green-house or conservatory.
CONDITIONING Stand in deep water for several hours.

Cobaea Cups and saucers
Climbing plants with large bell-shaped flowers of purple or pale green.
AVAILABILITY Summer and autumn.
PLANTING CONDITIONS As annuals in any soil against a sunny wall. Can be grown as perennials in greenhouse or conser-vatory to give longer season.
CONDITIONING Stand in deep water for several hours.

Conifers
A wide range of evergreen trees and shrubs to give all-year foliage for decoration. The cones are also decora-tive in some species.
AVAILABILITY All year.
PLANTING CONDITIONS Any soil. Sun or shade.
CONDITIONING Hammer stems, then stand in deep water for several hours.

Convallaria Lily-of-the-valley
Delicate little sprays of white bells of great charm. Excellent fragrance. A pink variety available. Good backing foliage. Last well in water. Good for forcing.
MEANING Unconscious sweetness; return of happiness.
AVAILABILITY Spring. Forced: all year.
PLANTING CONDITIONS Woodland condi-tions: any soil in shade.

CONDITIONING Stand in deep water for several hours.

Coreopsis
Yellow daisy-like flowers with darker yellow eyes. They generally have long stems and deeply divided leaves. Several cultivars available with dif-ferent shades of yellow and varying sizes of head and height.
MEANING Always cheerful.
AVAILABILITY Summer.
PLANTING CONDITIONS Any well-drained soil. Full sun.
CONDITIONING Stand in deep water for several hours.

Cornus Dogwood
A large range of shrubs with good bark for winter arrangements. White or yellow flowers and bracts in spring. Good autumn tints.
MEANING Durability.
AVAILABILITY Bark: all year, particularly winter. Flowers: spring. Tints: autumn.
PLANTING CONDITIONS Any soil. Sun or light shade.
CONDITIONING Hammer woody stems, dip stem ends in boiling water and then stand in deep water for several hours.

Corydalis
A genus of plants becoming very popu-lar but difficult to obtain except for *Corydalis lutea*. Small, delicate yellow flowers over filigree foliage.
AVAILABILITY Summer.
PLANTING CONDITIONS Any well-drained soil. Sun or shade. Grows well in walls.
CONDITIONING Stand in deep water for several hours.

Corylus Hazel
The familiar yellow catkins of lambs' tails of the hedgerow and coppice. The variety *C.* 'Contorta' has delightful twisted stems. Also purple-leaved variety which is good for foliage.
MEANING Reconciliation, peace.
AVAILABILITY Catkins: late winter, spring. Foliage: spring and summer.
PLANTING CONDITIONS Any soil. Sun.
CONDITIONING Hammer woody stems then stand in water for several hours.

Cosmos
Tall fresh-looking plants with feathery foliage and flowers of white, pink, red and orange. *C. atrosanguineus* has unusually dark brown flowers and smells of hot chocolate. Last quite well in water.
AVAILABILITY Summer and autumn.
PLANTING CONDITIONS Any soil. Sun.
CONDITIONING Stand in deep water for several hours.

Cotinus Smoke tree
Very valuable shrubs or trees with beautiful purple foliage. The leaves have a simple rounded shape which form a good background. Also have good autumn tints. Last reasonably well in water.
AVAILABILITY Summer and autumn.
PLANTING CONDITIONS Any soil. Full sun.

CONDITIONING Hammer woody stems, then stand in deep water for several hours.

Crocosmia Montbretia
Tall bulbous plants with sword-like leaves and arching sprays of bright orange flowers. Yellow varieties also available. Last quite well in water. Seed pods can be dried.
AVAILABILITY Late summer and autumn.
PLANTING CONDITIONS Any soil in sun.
CONDITIONING Stand in deep water for several hours.

Crocus
Small bulbous plants bearing flowers shaped like chalices. Colours vary from cream and bright orange to blue and mauve. Along with another similar genus, *Colchicum*, there are autumn forms.
MEANING Youthful gladness.
AVAILABILITY Late winter, spring and autumn.
PLANTING CONDITIONS Any soil. Full sun. Also as pot plants.

Cryptomeria Japanese cedar
Evergreen conifers with bronze, feath-ery foliage in winter and bright green foliage in spring. There are several varieties exhibiting different forms and colours of foliage.
AVAILABILITY All year.
PLANTING CONDITIONS All soils. Sun or light shade.
CONDITIONING Hammer woody stems, then stand in deep water for several hours.

Cucumis Melon
Round fruit from annual plants in green or yellow.
AVAILABILITY Autumn. All year from shops.
PLANTING CONDITIONS Greenhouse.

Cucurbita Gourds
Small decorative gourds grown like marrows with a variety of smooth and knobbly shapes. The predominant col-ours are yellow, orange and green.
MEANING Extent, bulkiness.
AVAILABILITY Autumn, but last through-out the year.
PLANTING CONDITIONS Good garden soil. Full sun. Train up a trellis or tripod.
CONDITIONING Dry, clean and then var-nish or polish with wax.

Cuphea Cigar flower
Small, drooping tubular flowers in a variety of bright reds and yellow. Suit-able for very tiny arrangements.
AVAILABILITY Summer.
PLANTING CONDITIONS As bedding plants in any soil, full sun or in a warm green-house or conservatory.

Cyclamen Sowbread
A number of delicate species which will give almost all-year-round flower-ing in greenhouse and open garden. Also larger, more blousy, florist cycla-men as indoor pot plants. Colours include white and purple. Pot plants

should not be over-watered.
MEANING Diffidence.
AVAILABILITY Species: autumn, winter and spring. Florists' plants: all year.
PLANTING CONDITIONS Species: well-drained soil in light shade. Florists' plants: greenhouse or conservatory, but prefer cool conditions.

Cymbidium
Aerial sprays of beautiful, exotic orchids in a large variety of colours with the exception of blue. Last extremely well in water.
AVAILABILITY All year from florists.
PLANTING CONDITIONS Warm green-house or conservatory.
CONDITIONING Stand in deep water for several hours.

Cynara Globe artichoke
Versatile plants with good foliage and flower-heads. The latter are large and thistle-like and can be used in bud, in flower or in seed. The leaves are evergreen.
AVAILABILITY Flower: autumn. Can also be used dried. Leaves: all year.
PLANTING CONDITIONS Any soil. Sun.
CONDITIONING Stand in deep water for several hours.

Cyperus Papyrus, umbrella plant
Plants with leaf-like bracts radiating from the top of the stem. Pot plants, but stems can be cut. Last well in water.
AVAILABILITY Summer.
PLANTING CONDITIONS Greenhouse or conservatory. Keep moist.
CONDITIONING Stand in deep water for several hours.

Cypripedium Slipper orchid
Curious orchids with slipper-like pouches, surmounted by waxed moustaches. Not so bright as some of the other orchids.
AVAILABILITY Summer.
PLANTING CONDITIONS Will grow outside in moist sheltered spot, but also cool greenhouse.
CONDITIONING Stand in deep water for several hours.

Cytisus Broom
Shrubs covered with masses of pea-like blooms. Available in white, yellow, orange, pink and red.
MEANING Humility, neatness.
AVAILABILITY Spring.
PLANTING CONDITIONS Any soil. Sun.
CONDITIONING Crush woody stems, boil, and then stand in deep water for several hours.

Dahlia
Half-hardy tuberous plants with a great variety in flower shape and colour. Col-ours include white, red, mauve, yellow and orange. Stems are long. They last well in water, particularly pompons.
MEANING Pomp.
AVAILABILITY Late summer and autumn.
PLANTING CONDITIONS Any soil in full sun.
CONDITIONING Stand in deep water for several hours.

Daphne
Small slow growing shrubs with fragrant flowers mainly in red, purple and white, also some in yellow. *D. laureola* is evergreen.
MEANING Painting the lily.
AVAILABILITY Late winter, spring and summer.
PLANTING CONDITIONS Any good, well-drained soil in full sun or light shade.
CONDITIONING Hammer woody stems, boil, then stand in deep water for several hours.

Delphinium
Tall spires of varying shades of spurred, blue flowers with a dark or white centre. Also white, pink and purple varieties available. Dwarf forms can now also be found. Seed-heads can be dried.
AVAILABILITY Summer, sometimes second flush in autumn.
PLANTING CONDITIONS Any good soil in full sun. Protect from winds.
CONDITIONING Fill hollow stems, then stand in deep water for several hours.

Deutzia
Shrubs with clusters of small single or double flowers in white or pink. Some of the double flowers are delightfully fringed. Last quite well in water.
AVAILABILITY Late spring and summer.
PLANTING CONDITIONS Any moisture-retentive soil. Full sun or light shade.
CONDITIONING Hammer woody stems, then stand in deep water for several hours.

Dianthus **Carnation, pink, sweet william**
One of the most popular of cut flowers. White, pink and red cultivars are available, some with a contrasting eye. Usually fragrant. All long lasting in water. Old-fashioned pinks and sweet williams have only a short season.
MEANING Carnations: fascination, woman's. Deep red – alas for my poor heart; striped – refusal; yellow – disdain. Pinks: boldness. Red – love; striped – refusal; white – talent.
AVAILABILITY Summer and autumn (old-fashioned pinks and sweet williams early summer only). All year from florists.
PLANTING CONDITIONS Any soil in sunny position. Some carnations in greenhouse only.
CONDITIONING Stand in deep water for several hours.

Dicentra **Bleeding heart**
Beautiful arching sprays of heart-shaped flowers with ferny foliage. Pink or white flowers. Last well in water.
AVAILABILITY Spring and summer.
PLANTING CONDITIONS Rich, moist soil. Light shade.
CONDITIONING Stand in deep water for several hours.

Digitalis **Foxglove**
These tall spires of purple bells are very evocative of high summer. There are varieties with bells all round the stems and other colours including white and yellow.
MEANING Insincerity.
AVAILABILITY Summer.
PLANTING CONDITIONS Any soil. Sun or light shade.
CONDITIONING Stand in deep water for several hours.

Diospyros **Persimmon**
A very decorative orange fruit.
MEANING Bury me amid nature's beauties.
AVAILABILITY Autumn.

Doronicum **Leopard's bane**
Golden yellow daisies that always seem to exude a freshness when they appear in spring. There are also double-flowered varieties.
AVAILABILITY Spring.
PLANTING CONDITIONS Any moisture-retentive soil. Sun or light shade.
CONDITIONING Stand in deep water for several hours.

Dryandra
Australian evergreen shrubs with orange and red flowers. Tender.
AVAILABILITY Spring.
PLANTING CONDITIONS Cool greenhouse or conservatory.
CONDITIONING Hammer woody stems then stand in deep water for several hours.

Echinops **Globe thistle**
Popular border plants with spiny spherical flowers much loved by bees. The commonest globe thistle has blue flowers but there are light green and white varieties. Tall and last very well in water.
AVAILABILITY Summer. But can also be used dried.
PLANTING CONDITIONS Any soil in full sun or partial shade.
CONDITIONING Stand in deep water for several hours.

Echium **Viper's bugloss**
Wild plants sometimes grown in gardens. Coils of blue flowers with red stamens. The leaves and stems are covered with small spines that get into the hands. Garden hybrids give a greater range of colours.
MEANING Falsehood.
AVAILABILITY Summer.
PLANTING CONDITIONS Any soil. Sun.
CONDITIONING Dip stem ends in boiling water, then stand in deep water for several hours.

Elaeagnus
Evergreen shrubs valuable for their foliage. *E. pungens* 'Maculata' and *E. × ebbingei* 'Gilt Edge' have excellent gold and green foliage and *E. angustifolia* and *E. commutata* have good silver foliage.
AVAILABILITY All year.
PLANTING CONDITIONS Any soil. Sun or light shade.
CONDITIONING Hammer woody stems then stand in deep water for several hours.

Epilobium **Willow herb**
Wild or garden plants with spires of dark rosy-red flowers. Some species have very tall stems. Wild forms can be a menace if grown in the garden.
MEANING Pretension.
AVAILABILITY Summer.
PLANTING CONDITIONS Any soil. Full sun.
CONDITIONING Dip stems in boiling water, then stand in deep water for several hours. Wilt unless dealt with straight after picking.

Eremurus **Foxtail lily**
Very tall, airy spikes of starlike flowers. Colours are white, pink or yellow. Some species are fragrant. Last well in water.
AVAILABILITY Summer.
PLANTING CONDITIONS Well-drained soil. Full sun and wind protection.
CONDITIONING Stand in deep water for several hours.

Erica **Heath**
Small shrubby plants useful both for the colour of their flowers and their foliage. There are always some varieties in flower all year. Flower colour varies from white to pink, mauve and purple. The leaves are of varying shades of green and gold. Even the rust brown seed-heads are attractive. Can be dried.
MEANING Solitude. White: good luck.
AVAILABILITY All year round.
PLANTING CONDITIONS Lime-free soil in full sun.
CONDITIONING Crush woody stems and then submerge in deep water for several hours.

Eryngium **Sea holly**
Very spiky but very decorative plants in which even the flowers have spines. Colours are mainly blue but there are also green and white varieties. Some are a very airy maze of branches, others are more compact.
AVAILABILITY Summer and autumn. Can also be used dried.
PLANTING CONDITIONS Any soil. Sun.
CONDITIONING Stand in deep water for several hours.

Escallonia
Late-flowering shrubs with arching stems covered with clusters of starry flowers in shades of pink, red and white. Glossy evergreen foliage. Last quite well in water.
AVAILABILITY Late summer and autumn.
PLANTING CONDITIONS Any soil. Full sun or light shade.
CONDITIONING Hammer woody stems, then stand in deep water for several hours.

Eucalyptus **Gum tree**
Very valuable for their evergreen greyish-silver foliage. Their very airy white flowers can also be attractive. Long lasting in water.
AVAILABILITY Foliage: all year. Flowers: late autumn, early winter.
PLANTING CONDITIONS Any soil. Sun.
CONDITIONING Hammer stems, then stand in deep water for several hours. Can also be preserved in glycerine.

Euonymus **Spindle**
The deciduous spindles are valuable for their autumn colour and their red berries which open like cardinals' hats. The evergreens are valuable for their glossy foliage of which there are good variegated forms.
MEANING Your charms are engraved upon my heart.
AVAILABILITY Autumn for tints and berries. All year for evergreen foliage.
PLANTING CONDITIONS Any soil. Sun or light shade.
CONDITIONING Hammer woody stems, then stand in deep water for several hours.

Euphorbia **Spurge**
Valuable yellow and green plants varying in height from short to tall. Long lasting in water. They also include the red-bracted poinsettia used as a pot plant. Exude a caustic white sap.
AVAILABILITY Spring and summer.
PLANTING CONDITIONS Any soil. Sun or partial shade.
CONDITIONING Staunch the sap with a naked flame or fine sand. Stand in deep water for several hours.

Eustoma **Prairie gentian**
Beautiful trumpets of purple flowers.
AVAILABILITY Summer from florists.
CONDITIONING Dip stem ends in boiling water, then stand in deep water for several hours.

Fagus **Beech**
Valuable shiny foliage in either green or purple. The nut capsules are an interesting shape and can also be useful.
MEANING Prosperity.
AVAILABILITY Foliage: spring and summer. Fruit: autumn.
PLANTING CONDITIONS Any soil. Sun or light shade.
CONDITIONING Hammer woody stems, then stand in deep water for several hours. Can be preserved with glycerine.

Fatsia
Large, glossy, dark green leaves, deeply lobed like the fingers on a hand. Valuable for foliage decorations. Long lasting in water.
AVAILABILITY Summer.
PLANTING CONDITIONS Any soil. Full or partial shade.
CONDITIONING Crush woody stems and then stand in deep water for several hours. Can also be preserved in glycerine.

Ferns
A wide range of shapes and textures; some filigree, others strap-like. The fronds also have quite a range of different greens. They last well in water after cutting.
MEANING Fascination.
AVAILABILITY Spring to autumn.

PLANTING CONDITIONS Moist, shady positions.
CONDITIONING Char stem ends with naked flame and stand in deep water for several hours.

Ficus **Rubber plant, weeping fig**
Foliage plants with glossy, leathery leaves of different sizes. Some useful for cutting. Also used as pot plants.
AVAILABILITY All year.
PLANTING CONDITIONS Warm greenhouse or conservatory.
CONDITIONING Boil stem ends, then stand in deep water for several hours.

Forsythia **Golden-bell**
Shrubs with starry yellow flowers which are out just before the leaves appear. Can be cut in winter for forcing long before the flowers normally appear. Last quite well in water.
AVAILABILITY Spring. Winter if forced.
PLANTING CONDITIONS Any soil. Sun or light shade.
CONDITIONING Hammer woody stems, then stand in deep water for several hours.

Fragaria **Strawberry**
Bright red strawberries can be used for short-lived displays. Small alpine strawberries still attached to stems with leaves and flowers are also attractive.
MEANING Perfect excellence.
AVAILABILITY Summer.
PLANTING CONDITIONS Rich soil. Full sun.
CONDITIONING Avoid eating.

Freesia
One of the most scented of cut flowers. The stems of waxy flowers open one or two at a time. The upward-facing trumpets are available in a wide variety of colours. They last well in water.
AVAILABILITY Summer. All year from florists.
PLANTING CONDITIONS Will grow outside but greenhouse culture advisable.
CONDITIONING Stand in deep water for several hours.

Fritillaria **Fritillary, crown imperial**
A large genus of bulbous plants, the most common being the snake's-head fritillary with its solitary, nodding purple or white checkered bells. Crown imperials are much larger with a cluster of yellow or orange-red bells on the top of the stem, surmounted by leaves looking like a pineapple.
MEANING Majesty, power.
AVAILABILITY Spring.
PLANTING CONDITIONS Moist soil. Sun.
CONDITIONING Stand in deep water for several hours.

Fuchsia
Small shrubs with pendulous flowers, usually bell-shaped, in a range of pinks, purples and reds. Some forms have variegated foliage. Only a few are hardy.
MEANING Scarlet: taste.
AVAILABILITY Summer and autumn.

PLANTING CONDITIONS Any soil. Sun. Greenhouse for the tender species.
CONDITIONING Crush woody stems, boil ends, and then stand in deep water for several hours.

Gaillardia **Blanket flower**
Brash daisy-like flowers in glowing shades of red, yellow and orange. Double and single forms. Last well in water.
AVAILABILITY Summer and autumn.
PLANTING CONDITIONS Any soil. Full sun.
CONDITIONING Stand in deep water for several hours.

Garrya **Silk tassel bush**
Valuable evergreen shrubs that have flowers in the form of long, silky, green tassels throughout the winter when there is not much else around. Last well in water.
AVAILABILITY Winter.
PLANTING CONDITIONS Any soil; sun or shade.
CONDITIONING Hammer woody stems, then stand in deep water for several hours.

Genista **Broom**
Arching branches of yellow pea-shaped flowers. Some species are fragrant. Last quite well in water.
MEANING Humility, neatness.
AVAILABILITY Early summer.
PLANTING CONDITIONS Well-drained soil. Full sun.
CONDITIONING Crush woody stems and then stand in deep water for several hours.

Gentiana **Gentian**
Upright trumpets of bright blue. The majority are short-stemmed but there are some bigger subjects, such as *G. asclepiadea*, which is up to 60cm (2ft). Some species have whitish varieties.
AVAILABILITY Spring to late autumn.
PLANTING CONDITIONS *G. asclepiadea* and *G. sino-ornata* prefer moist rootrun; others well-drained soil. All species prefer sun.
CONDITIONING Stand in a warm, light place to open fully.

Geranium **Cranesbill**
Popular herbaceous perennials with saucer-shaped flowers. There is a vast number of species available in colours ranging from the basic blue, mauve and purple, to red, pink and white, many having contrasting veining. Vary in height from small to tall. Not long lasting.
MEANING Steadfast pity.
AVAILABILITY Summer and autumn.
PLANTING CONDITIONS Well-drained soil. Mainly sun, though some prefer light shade.
CONDITIONING Stand in deep water for several hours.

Gerbera **Transvaal daisy**
Brightly coloured, daisy-like flowers in cream, yellow, orange, red, pink or purple. Tender. Last well in water.

AVAILABILITY All year.
PLANTING CONDITIONS Greenhouse cultivation.
CONDITIONING Boil stem ends, then stand in deep water for several hours.

Geum **Avens**
Herbaceous perennials with brilliant red, yellow or orange flowers. There are single, semi-double or double flowers, the general shape being circular. Tend to hang their heads.
AVAILABILITY Late spring and summer.
PLANTING CONDITIONS Any soil. Sunny position.
CONDITIONING Boil stem ends, then stand in deep water for several hours before using.

Gladiolus **Sword lily**
These are well-known bulbous plants with tall, slightly arching stems of brightly coloured flowers. The leaves are long and sword-like. Most colours are available except true blue. Last well in water.
AVAILABILITY Summer and autumn.
PLANTING CONDITIONS Any soil. Full sun.
CONDITIONING Remove top buds, crush stems and then stand in deep water for several hours.

Glaucium **Horned-poppy**
Bright yellow or orange-red, papery flowers set off against a greyish stem and foliage. Long curved seed pods from whence comes its English name.
AVAILABILITY Summer and autumn.
PLANTING CONDITIONS Well-drained soil. Full sun.
CONDITIONING Stand in deep water for several hours.

Gomphrena
Of the many species *G. globosa* is the main one in cultivation. Annuals with globular flowers of white, yellow, orange, red, pink and purple. Flowers are "everlasting" and can be dried.
AVAILABILITY Summer.
PLANTING CONDITIONS Any soil. Full sun. Or as pot plants in greenhouse.
CONDITIONING Stand in deep water for several hours.

Grevillea
Tender shrubs important for their evergreen, fern-like foliage and bright petal-less flowers in yellow and red. Last well when cut.
AVAILABILITY Summer.
PLANTING CONDITIONS Greenhouse and conservatory in lime-free soil.
CONDITIONING Crush woody stems and stand in deep water for several hours. Can be preserved in glycerine.

Griselinia
Evergreen shrubs valuable for their foliage, particularly in variegated forms. Long lasting.
AVAILABILITY All year.
PLANTING CONDITIONS Well-drained soil. Sun or light shade.
CONDITIONING Crush woody stems and then stand in deep water for several hours.

Gypsophila **Baby's breath**
Marvellous airy plants with fine wiry stems and little puffs of dainty white flowers. Pink varieties also available. Long lasting in water.
AVAILABILITY Summer. Can also be used dried.
PLANTING CONDITIONS Well-drained soil. Full sun.
CONDITIONING Stand in deep water for several hours.

Hamamelis **Witch hazel**
Deciduous shrubs with flowers made up of clusters of spidery, strap-like yellow petals on the naked branches. The flowers are fragrant.
MEANING A spell, a charm.
AVAILABILITY Late winter.
PLANTING CONDITIONS Lime-free soil. Sun or light shade.
CONDITIONING Hammer woody stems then stand in deep water for several hours.

Hebe **Shrubby veronica**
A group of mainly New Zealand evergreen shrubs with dense spikes of blue, white or pink flowers. Some are scented. A few species are hardy; the rest need winter protection.
AVAILABILITY Summer and autumn.
PLANTING CONDITIONS Any soil. Full sun.
CONDITIONING Crush woody stems, boil stem ends, and then stand in deep water for several hours.

Hedera **Ivy**
Creeping foliage plants with distinctive leaves. There is considerable variation in size of leaf and the markings found on them. There are many variegated forms. Long lasting. Also available as pot plants.
MEANING Fidelity, marriage.
AVAILABILITY All year.
PLANTING CONDITIONS Any soil. Sun or shade. Must have some support.
CONDITIONING Crush woody stems, and then stand in deep water for several hours.

Helenium **Sneezeweed**
Clusters of yellow, daisy-like flowers on top of medium-length stems. Orange and brown varieties also available. Last quite well in water.
MEANING Tears.
AVAILABILITY Summer and autumn.
PLANTING CONDITIONS Any soil. Sun.
CONDITIONING Crush woody stems and then stand in deep water for several hours.

Helianthus **Sunflower**
Very tall, yellow daisy-like flowers. The well-known annual sunflower has a large, dark central disc. The perennial flowers are all much smaller.
MEANING Short: adoration. Tall: haughtiness.
AVAILABILITY Autumn.
PLANTING CONDITIONS Rich soil. Full sun.
CONDITIONING Dip stem ends into boiling water, and then stand in deep water for several hours.

Helichrysum Everlasting flower
Very colourful daisy-like flowers with papery bracts instead of petals. They can be yellow, brown, orange, red or pink. Last very well and extremely good dried.
AVAILABILITY Summer. Also used dried.
PLANTING CONDITIONS Any soil. Full sun.
CONDITIONING Stand in deep water for several hours.

Helleborus Christmas rose, Lenten rose, hellebore
An interesting range of saucer-shaped, winter flowers varying in colour from the white Christmas rose to the plum coloured and spotted Lenten roses. The green and stinking hellebores have smaller, more cup-shaped flowers.
MEANING Scandal, calumny.
AVAILABILITY Winter and spring.
PLANTING CONDITIONS Moist, rich soil. Shady position.
CONDITIONING Prick the stems with a pin and submerge in water for several hours.

Heracleum Giant hogweed
Very tall plants with cartwheels of white flowers, like giant cow parsley. Sap can cause skin irritation. Seed-heads can be used dried.
AVAILABILITY Late summer.
PLANTING CONDITIONS Any soil. Sun or light shade.
CONDITIONING Boil stem ends, then stand in deep water for several hours.

Heuchera Coral flower
Sprays of airy flowers on thin stems. Colours include white, cream, pink and red. Last quite well in water.
AVAILABILITY Summer.
PLANTING CONDITIONS Any soil. Sun or light shade.
CONDITIONING Stand in deep water for several hours. Float leaves on water.

Hibiscus
Exotic trumpet-shaped flowers borne on tender shrubs and perennials. Each flower lasts only a day, and is then replaced by more. Full range of tropical colours.
MEANING Delicate beauty.
AVAILABILITY Late summer, autumn.
PLANTING CONDITIONS Greenhouse or conservatory culture.
CONDITIONING Crush woody stems, and then stand in deep water for several hours.

Hippeastrum Amaryllis
Large lily-type flowers radiating from a tall stem. White, pink or red. Strap-like leaves. Bulbous.
MEANING Splendid beauty.
AVAILABILITY Winter, spring.
PLANTING CONDITIONS Tender pot plants for greenhouse or conservatory.
CONDITIONING Fill hollow stem with water and stand in deep water for several hours. If head is heavy, support with cane pushed up hollow stem.

Hosta Plantain lily
Marvellous for both their foliage and

arching spikes of flowers. The leaves are large and heart-shaped in varying shades of green and steely blue. There are also many variegated forms. The flowers are either white, lilac-blue or purple. Long lasting in water.
AVAILABILITY Summer, autumn.
PLANTING CONDITIONS Moist rich soil. Shade but will tolerate sun.
CONDITIONING Submerge leaves, then stand in deep water for several more hours.

Hyacinthoides Bluebell
Arching stems of blue bells and glossy, strap-like leaves. Also pink and white varieties available. Fragrant.
MEANING Constancy, kindness.
AVAILABILITY Spring.
PLANTING CONDITIONS Woodland conditions of moist soil and shade, but will take full sun.
CONDITIONING Stand in deep water for several hours.

Hyacinthus Hyacinth
Bulbous plants with spikes of very fragrant flowers in blue, white and pink. Can be used as pot plants.
MEANING Sport, game, play. White: unobtrusive loveliness.
AVAILABILITY Spring. Winter if forced.
PLANTING CONDITIONS Any soil. Sun or light shade.
CONDITIONING Stand in deep water for several hours. Support stems with inside wires.

Hydrangea
Shrubs with large mops of flower-heads. White, blue, mauve, pink and red. There are also varieties with pointed spikes of flowers and delicate lacecaps, with just a few large, sterile florets round the edge of tiny, fertile florets.
MEANING A boaster, heartlessness.
AVAILABILITY Summer, autumn.
PLANTING CONDITIONS Deep, rich, moist soil. Light shade.
CONDITIONING Float heads, then stand in deep water for several more hours.

Hypericum St John's wort
Shrubs and sub-shrubs with saucer-shaped, golden-yellow flowers. Several good fruiting forms including *H. calycinum* (rose of sharon).
MEANING Animosity, superstition.
AVAILABILITY Summer and autumn.
PLANTING CONDITIONS Any soil. Light shade or sun.
CONDITIONING Crush stems, and stand in deep water for several hours.

Iberis Candytuft
Flat or domed heads of white flowers. Also pink and mauve varieties. Short-stemmed. Last very well in water. Seed-heads can be dried.
MEANING Indifference.
AVAILABILITY Spring.
PLANTING CONDITIONS Any soil. Sun or light shade.
CONDITIONING Stand in deep water for several hours.

Ilex Holly
Glossy prickly-leaved shrubs or trees useful for their foliage and bright red berries borne in mid-winter. There are variegated and yellow-berried forms. Flowers are insignificant. Last well in water. Used particularly at Christmas time.
MEANING Foresight.
AVAILABILITY Winter.
PLANTING CONDITIONS Any soil. Sun or shade.
CONDITIONING Hammer woody stems, then stand in deep water for several hours.

Iris Flag
Flowers that cover a long season starting with *I. unguicularis* just before Christmas, followed by the Reticulatas in winter and spring, and finally the taller species in summer. Some are scented.
MEANING Message.
AVAILABILITY Winter, spring and summer. All year from florists.
PLANTING CONDITIONS Well-drained soil. Sun. Reticulatas can be grown as pot plants.
CONDITIONING Stand in deep water for several hours. Remove dead flowers as they appear.

Ixia
Slender-stemmed bulbous plants with several star-like flowers per stem. A large range of colours including bluish-green. Last well in water. Tender except in milder parts.
AVAILABILITY Spring.
PLANTING CONDITIONS Well-drained soil. Full sun.
CONDITIONING Stand in deep water for several hours.

Jasminum Jasmine
Both winter and summer forms. The former has starry yellow flowers on arching stems. In the summer there are white forms which are very fragrant. There are also yellow and pink forms in summer. Winter forms last better in water.
MEANING White: amiability. Yellow: grace and elegance.
AVAILABILITY Winter, summer.
PLANTING CONDITIONS Any soil. Sun or shade.
CONDITIONING Stand in deep water for several hours immediately after cutting stems.

Juniperus Juniper
Columnar or spreading evergreen conifers giving all-year-round foliage. Colour varies from green and blue to gold. The dwarf *J. communis* 'Compressa' is small enough for the whole tree to be used if potted.
MEANING Succour, protection.
AVAILABILITY All year.
PLANTING CONDITIONS Any soil. Sun or shade.
CONDITIONING Hammer woody stems, then stand in deep water for several hours.

Kalanchoe
Tender succulents grown as pot plants which flower throughout the year. Flowers can be white, pink, red or yellow.
AVAILABILITY All year.
PLANTING CONDITIONS Pot plants in greenhouse or conservatory.

Kniphofia Red-hot poker, torch lily
Tall upright stems with a colourful spike of red, orange or yellow flowers. Not long lasting in water.
AVAILABILITY Summer, autumn.
PLANTING CONDITIONS Any soil. Full sun.
CONDITIONING Stand in deep water for several hours.

Kochia Burning bush
Fine-leaved plants that resemble herbaceous· "busbies". They are bright green turning dark red in autumn. Can be grown in pots.
AVAILABILITY Summer and autumn.
PLANTING CONDITIONS Any soil. Sun.

Laburnum Golden chain, golden rain
Trees with long pendulous tassels of yellow pea-like flowers.
MEANING Forsaken, pensive beauty.
AVAILABILITY Early summer.
PLANTING CONDITIONS All soils. Sun.
CONDITIONING Put stems in boiling water, then stand in deep water for several hours.

Lachenalia Cape cowslip
Tender bulbous plants with a spike of numerous bell-shaped flowers in red, yellow and orange. Last well in water. Can be used as pot plants.
AVAILABILITY Winter and spring.
PLANTING CONDITIONS Pot plants for warm greenhouse or conservatory.
CONDITIONING Stand in deep water for several hours.

Larix Larch
Deciduous conifers best in spring when the light green, new growth is supplemented by the newly forming cones which are pink or red. Branches with sprays of small cones can be used in winter.
MEANING Audacity, boldness.
AVAILABILITY Foliage: spring. Cones: winter.
PLANTING CONDITIONS Any soil. Sunny position.
CONDITIONING Hammer woody stems, then stand in deep water for several hours.

Lathyrus Everlasting pea, sweet pea
Sweet peas are justly well loved for their grace and fresh smell. There is now a vast range of cultivars from which to choose. Not all are fragrant. The long-stemmed flowers last quite well in water. There are also many other species which are perennial but these lack scent and have restricted colour range.
MEANING Delicate pleasures, departure.
AVAILABILITY Summer.

PLANTING CONDITIONS Rich, well-drained soil. Full sun.
CONDITIONING Stand in deep water for several hours.

Lavandula **Lavender**
Grey-leaved shrubs with spikes of pale purple flowers on long stems. The plants are very strongly scented. There are darker purple and white forms. Can be dried.
MEANING Distrust.
AVAILABILITY Summer and autumn.
PLANTING CONDITIONS Any soil. Sunny position.
CONDITIONING Stand in deep water for several hours.

Lavatera **Mallow**
Annuals with bright pink or white trumpets. Also perennial species but these are duller and not so interesting. Last reasonably well in water after cutting.
MEANING Mildness.
AVAILABILITY Summer and autumn.
PLANTING CONDITIONS Any soil. Sunny position.
CONDITIONING Dip ends in boiling water, then stand in deep water for several hours.

Leptospermum **Manuka, tea tree**
Increasingly popular New Zealand shrubs for the milder parts of the country. Branches covered with masses of small white, pink or red flowers.
AVAILABILITY Summer.
PLANTING CONDITIONS Well-drained soil. Full sun. Winter protection needed.
CONDITIONING Hammer woody stems, then stand in deep water for several hours.

Liatris **Gayfeather**
Several species of long purple spikes of feathery flowers. Unusual in that they flower from tip of spike downwards. Last well in water.
AVAILABILITY Summer and autumn.
PLANTING CONDITIONS Any soil. Sun.
CONDITIONING Stand in deep water for several hours.

Ligustrum **Privet**
Evergreen shrubs useful for their foliage. Available in golden colours as well as green. White flowers with a scent that some find nasty, others attractive. Black berries in autumn.
MEANING Prohibition.
AVAILABILITY All year.
PLANTING CONDITIONS Any soil. Sun or light shade.
CONDITIONING Hammer woody stems, then stand in deep water for several hours.

Lilium **Lily**
Beautiful, well-loved flowers shaped either like large trumpets or turks' caps with curled back petals. Large range of colours (except blue), either plain or spotted. Many are fragrant. Last very well in water.
MEANING Regal: majesty. White: purity, sweetness. Yellow: falsehood, gaiety.
AVAILABILITY Summer and autumn. All

year from florists.
PLANTING CONDITIONS Well-drained soil. Sun or light shade.
CONDITIONING Stand in deep water for several hours.

Limonium **Sea lavender, statice**
Brightly coloured flowers that last very well in water. A large range of colours available with blue, yellow and pink predominating.
MEANING Dauntlessness.
AVAILABILITY Summer and autumn. All year from florists.
PLANTING CONDITIONS Any soil. Sunny position.
CONDITIONING Stand in deep water for several hours.

Lonicera **Honeysuckle**
Well-known and well-loved climbing plants which produce very heavily scented flowers, particularly strong in the evening. There are various colours available, including yellow, orange and red. There are also variegated-leaved forms. Do not last very long in water after cutting.
MEANING Generous and devoted affection.
AVAILABILITY Summer and autumn.
PLANTING CONDITIONS Any soil. Sun or light shade.
CONDITIONING Stand in deep water for several hours.

Lunaria **Honesty**
Biennial and perennial plants that do double service. In spring they have purple or white flowers. There are varieties with good variegated foliage. Later they have almost transparent, silky seed-cases that are extremely useful in dried arrangements.
MEANING Honesty, fascination.
AVAILABILITY Flowers: spring. Seed-cases: autumn.
PLANTING CONDITIONS Any soil. Sun or shade.
CONDITIONING Stand in deep water for several hours. Dry on the plant and remove outer scales.

Lupinus **Lupin**
Old-fashioned, cottage garden plants with spires of pea-like flowers. Large number of cultivars available in a good range of colours including yellow, blue, white, pink and orange. Peppery scent. Last very well in water.
MEANING Voraciousness.
AVAILABILITY Summer.
PLANTING CONDITIONS Any soil. Full sun.
CONDITIONING Fill hollow stems and plug. Stand in deep water for several hours.

Lysimachia **Yellow loosestrife**
Spikes of bright yellow, cup-shaped flowers. The spikes are clothed with whorls of flowers backed by leaves. Last quite well in water.
AVAILABILITY Summer.
PLANTING CONDITIONS Any soil, preferably moist. Sun or light shade.
CONDITIONING Stand in deep water for several hours.

Lythrum **Purple loosestrife**
Tall herbaceous plants that have spires of brilliant purple flowers. They do not last very long in water but add a good vertical emphasis, with a splash of strong colour, to arrangements.
AVAILABILITY Late summer and autumn.
PLANTING CONDITIONS Prefer moist soil. Full sun.
CONDITIONING Boil stem ends, then stand in deep water for several hours.

Magnolia
Deciduous and evergreen shrubs and trees with predominantly white flowers, sometimes flushed with pink. Some are scented.
MEANING Love of nature.
AVAILABILITY Spring and summer.
PLANTING CONDITIONS Any soil except extreme alkaline. Sun or light shade.
CONDITIONING Hammer woody stems then dip in boiling water and stand in deep water for several hours.

Mahonia **Oregon grape**
Evergreen shrubs with glossy, spiny leaves and spikes of fragrant yellow flowers. Blue-black fruit in autumn.
AVAILABILITY Foliage: all year. Flowers: winter, spring. Fruit: autumn.
PLANTING CONDITIONS Any soil. Sun or light shade.
CONDITIONING Hammer woody stems, then stand in deep water for several hours.

Malus **Apple, crab apple**
Deciduous trees with pink-tinged blossom in spring, and shiny green, yellow or red apples of various sizes in the autumn. Some have decorative foliage.
MEANING Temptation.
AVAILABILITY Blossom: spring. Foliage: summer, autumn. Fruit: autumn.
PLANTING CONDITIONS Any soil. Sun.
CONDITIONING Hammer woody stems, then stand in deep water for several hours.

Matthiola **Stock**
Annuals and biennials, which are among the most popular cut flowers, with small spired, soft-coloured, scented flowers. Good range of pink, purple, white, yellow and cream. Last quite well in water.
MEANING Lasting beauty.
AVAILABILITY Summer. Florists: spring and summer.
PLANTING CONDITIONS Any soil. Sunny position.
CONDITIONING Stand in deep water for several hours.

Miscanthus
Tall ornamental grasses valuable for their foliage and plumed seed-heads. Several variegated forms including one with horizontal yellow stripes on the leaves.
AVAILABILITY Summer. Can also be used dried.
PLANTING CONDITIONS Any soil. Sun or light shade.

CONDITIONING Stand in deep water for several hours.

Molucella **Bells of Ireland, shell flower**
Tall stems of green trumpets in which sit tiny white flowers. The green calyces continue long after the flower dies. Last very well in water.
AVAILABILITY Summer and autumn. Can also be used dried.
PLANTING CONDITIONS Any soil in sunny position.
CONDITIONING Stand in deep water for several hours.

Monarda **Bergamot**
Whorls of red, pink or white flowers that seem to spring from a pincushion at the top of the stem. Very aromatic foliage when crushed.
AVAILABILITY Summer and autumn.
PLANTING CONDITIONS Moisture-retentive soil. Full sun.
CONDITIONING Stand in deep water for several hours.

Muscari **Grape hyacinth**
Small-stemmed bulbs with spikes of varying shades of blue flowers. Scented. White varieties also available.
AVAILABILITY Spring.
PLANTING CONDITIONS Any soil. Sun or light shade.
CONDITIONING Stand in deep water for several hours.

Myosotis **Forget-me-not**
Short arching sprays of blue flowers. Last quite well in water.
MEANING True love, forget-me-not.
AVAILABILITY Late spring, summer.
PLANTING CONDITIONS Any soil. Sun or light shade.
CONDITIONING Stand in deep water for several hours. Keep cool.

Narcissus **Daffodil, jonquil**
Very popular spring bulbs with trumpets or cups coming from a disc of petals. Mainly yellow but also white, orange and pink. There are many forms of miniature daffodil including the jonquils. Many are fragrant.
MEANING Regard.
AVAILABILITY Spring. Florists: winter and spring.
PLANTING CONDITIONS Any soil.
CONDITIONING Cut in bud. Stand in deep water for several hours.

Nepeta **Catmint**
Airy stems of pale blue or mauve flowers set off against grey foliage. The foliage is fragrant, particularly when crushed. Last quite well in water.
AVAILABILITY Summer.
PLANTING CONDITIONS Any soil. Full sun.
CONDITIONING Stand in deep water for several hours.

Nephrolepis **Ladder fern**
Evergreen ferns that are usually grown as pot plants. The cut fronds last well in water.

AVAILABILITY All year.
PLANTING CONDITIONS Greenhouse or conservatory.
CONDITIONING Stand in deep water for several hours.

Nerine
Autumnal bulbous plants with clusters of pink trumpet-like flowers. Last very well in water.
AVAILABILITY Autumn.
PLANTING CONDITIONS Any soil. Full sun; sheltered position. Not hardy in very cold areas.
CONDITIONING Stand in deep water for several hours.

Nicotiana **Tobacco plant**
Annual starry-flowered plants coming in a variety of colours, the greens being particularly important. Some varieties very fragrant, particularly after dark. Last well in water.
AVAILABILITY Summer and autumn.
PLANTING CONDITIONS Any soil. Sun.
CONDITIONING Stand in deep water for several hours.

Nigella **Love-in-a-mist**
Hardy annuals with blue flowers and a collar of bright-green, feathery foliage. Last very well in water.
MEANING Perplexity.
AVAILABILITY Summer.
PLANTING CONDITIONS Any soil. Sun. Self-seeding.
CONDITIONING Stand in deep water for several hours.

Ornithogalum **Chincherinchee, star of Bethlehem**
Bulbs with either sprays or spikes of small white flowers. Last very well in water.
AVAILABILITY Spring. All year from florists.
PLANTING CONDITIONS Any soil. Sun. Some need greenhouse protection.
CONDITIONING Stand in deep water for several hours.

Osmunda **Flowering fern, royal fern**
Tall deciduous ferns.
AVAILABILITY Summer.
PLANTING CONDITIONS Rich moist soil. Sun or light shade.
CONDITIONING Stand in deep water for several hours.

Paeonia **Paeony**
Herbaceous or shrubby plants. Large bold flower-heads of white, yellow, pink or red. Can be single or double. Some scented.
MEANING Shame, bashfulness.
AVAILABILITY Summer.
PLANTING CONDITIONS Any rich soil. Light shade.
CONDITIONING Stand in deep water for several hours.

Papaver **Poppy**
Brightly coloured flowers with tissue-like petals. Not long lasting in water.
MEANING Red: consolation. Scarlet:

fantastic extravagance. White: sleep.
AVAILABILITY Summer and autumn.
PLANTING CONDITIONS Any soil. Full sun.
CONDITIONING Cut as buds open. Seal sappy stem over naked flame or in boiling water.

Pelargonium **Geranium**
Tender plants with very colourful heads of flowers in bright reds, pinks, purples and white. Some leaves are fragrant and others have good zonal markings.
MEANING Dark: melancholy. Ivy: bridal preference. Scarlet: comforting, stupidity.
AVAILABILITY Summer and autumn.
PLANTING CONDITIONS Any soil. Sun. Over-winter protection needed.
CONDITIONING Stand in deep water for several hours.

Penstemon
Spikes of tubular flowers of bright or subtle colours. Available in a range of red, pink, purple and blue. Do not last long in water.
AVAILABILITY Summer and autumn.
PLANTING CONDITIONS Any well-drained soil. Sun.
CONDITIONING Stand in deep water for several hours.

Pernettya **Prickly heath**
Low shrubs with small bell-shaped flowers, but it is the mass of round berries which clothe the stems that are most useful in arrangements. They come in a range of colours: white, pink and red. They are evergreen with small leaves.
AVAILABILITY Flowers: summer. Berries: autumn.
PLANTING CONDITIONS Acid soil only. Full sun.
CONDITIONING Hammer woody stems, then stand in deep water for several hours.

Peucedanum **Hog's fennel**
Flat heads of white, yellow or pink flowers.
AVAILABILITY Summer.
PLANTING CONDITIONS Any soil. Sun or light shade.
CONDITIONING Stand in deep water for several hours.

Phaseolus **Bean**
Climbing plants with white, red, purple or yellow, pea-like flowers.
AVAILABILITY Summer and autumn.
PLANTING CONDITIONS Any soil. Sun.
CONDITIONING Stand in deep water for several hours.

Philadelphus **Mock orange**
Hardy shrubs with heavily scented white flowers. There are double-flowered and golden-leaved forms.
MEANING Counterfeit.
AVAILABILITY Summer.
PLANTING CONDITIONS Any soil. Sun or light shade.
CONDITIONING Remove most of the leaves. Hammer woody stems then stand in deep water for several hours.

Phlomis **Jerusalem sage**
Whorls of yellow sage-like flowers with soft felty leaves.
AVAILABILITY Summer.
PLANTING CONDITIONS Any soil. Sun.
CONDITIONING Crush stems and stand in deep water for several hours.

Phlox
Tall border plants with large heads of brightly coloured flowers in white, blue, pink, red and mauve. Last well.
MEANING Unanimity.
AVAILABILITY Summer.
PLANTING CONDITIONS Sun or shade. Moisture-retentive soil.
CONDITIONING Crush woody stems and then stand in deep water for several hours.

Physalis **Cape gooseberry, Chinese lantern**
It is the bright orange paper lanterns that enclose the fruit which make these plants decorative. They can be used fresh or dried.
AVAILABILITY Autumn. Also used dried.
PLANTING CONDITIONS Well-drained soil. Sun.
CONDITIONING Pick when colour begins to show. Remove leaves. Stand in deep water for several hours.

Picea **Spruce**
Evergreen conifers used for their foliage, particularly as Christmas trees.
AVAILABILITY All year.
PLANTING CONDITIONS Any soil. Sun.
CONDITIONING Hammer woody stems, then stand in deep water for several hours.

Pieris
Evergreen shrubs with masses of lily-of-the-valley flowers hanging in bunches. The shiny young foliage is red in spring.
AVAILABILITY Spring.
PLANTING CONDITIONS Lime-free soil. Light shade.
CONDITIONING Hammer woody stems, then stand in deep water for several hours.

Pinus **Pine**
Evergreen conifers with needle-like leaves in bunches and cones. Good for winter arrangements.
MEANING Pity.
AVAILABILITY All year.
PLANTING CONDITIONS Acid soils. Sun.
CONDITIONING Hammer woody stems, then stand in deep water for several hours.

Pittosporum
Evergreen shrubs with useful shiny foliage. There are variegated and purple forms. Last well in water.
AVAILABILITY All year.
PLANTING CONDITIONS Well-drained soil.
CONDITIONING Hammer woody stems, then stand in deep water for several hours.

Platycodon **Balloon flower**
Called balloon flowers because of their

interesting shape while in bud, when the flowers resemble inflated balloons. The flower itself is like a large open campanula in a rich blue. Also white forms.
AVAILABILITY Summer.
PLANTING CONDITIONS Any soil. Full sun.
CONDITIONING Dip stems in boiling water, then stand in deep water for several hours.

Polemonium **Jacob's ladder**
Spikes of white or blue, saucer-shaped flowers.
MEANING Come down.
AVAILABILITY Late spring and summer.
PLANTING CONDITIONS Any soil. Sun or light shade.
CONDITIONING Stand in deep water for several hours.

Polianthes **Tuberose**
White-flowered, bulbous plants with very strong scent. Tender.
MEANING Dangerous pleasures.
AVAILABILITY Summer. All year from florists.
PLANTING CONDITIONS Greenhouse or conservatory.
CONDITIONING Stand in deep water for several hours.

Polygonatum **Solomon's seal**
Graceful arching stems with small white bells hanging below the outstretched leaves. Very cool appearance. Last quite well in water.
AVAILABILITY Spring and early summer.
PLANTING CONDITIONS Moist woodland soil. Shade.
CONDITIONING Stand in deep water for several hours.

Polygonum **Bistort, snakeweed**
Small or medium stems of pink or red flowers. Still look good when they have turned brown. Last well in water.
AVAILABILITY Summer and autumn.
PLANTING CONDITIONS Any soil. Sun or light shade.
CONDITIONING Dip stems in boiling water, then stand in deep water for several hours.

Populus **Poplar**
Deciduous trees or shrubs with shiny heart-shaped leaves. Silver and gold forms available. Flowers of no importance.
MEANING Black: courage. White: time.
AVAILABILITY Summer.
PLANTING CONDITIONS Any soil. Sun or light shade.
CONDITIONING Hammer woody stems, then stand in deep water for several hours.

Primula **Auricula, cowslip, polyanthus, primrose**
Short-stemmed flowers, mainly yellow, but other bright colours available. Many fragrant.
MEANING Cowslip: pensiveness, winning grace. Polyanthus: pride of riches. Primrose: early youth.
AVAILABILITY Spring. Winter as pot plants.

PLANTING CONDITIONS Any soil. Light shade.
CONDITIONING Stand in deep water for several hours.

Protea
Tender shrubs with large flower-heads of differing shapes in red, pink, white, yellow, orange and purple. They last a very long time in water and can be used dried.
AVAILABILITY All year round from florists.
PLANTING CONDITIONS Greenhouse or conservatory.
CONDITIONING Hammer woody stems, then stand in deep water for several hours.

Prunus **Almond, cherry, peach, plum**
Trees or shrubs bearing pink or white blossom. Many varieties have double flowers. Some flower very early. Do not last long in water.
MEANING Cherry: good education. Plum: fidelity.
AVAILABILITY Mainly spring, but also winter.
PLANTING CONDITIONS Any soil. Sunny position.
CONDITIONING Hammer woody stems, then stand in deep water for several hours.

Pulmonaria **Lungwort**
Blue, purple, pink or red flowers on low growing border plant. Some varieties have silver, variegated or spotted leaves.
AVAILABILITY Spring, but also some in winter.
PLANTING CONDITIONS Shade. Moisture-retentive soil.
CONDITIONING Stand in deep water for several hours.

Punica **Pomegranate**
A spherical fruit with a yellowish-red or brown skin.
MEANING Foolishness.
AVAILABILITY Autumn from green-grocers.

Pyrethrum
Daisy-like flowers in bright colours: red, pink and white. Feathery foliage. Last quite well in water.
AVAILABILITY Summer and autumn.
PLANTING CONDITIONS Any soil. Sun.
CONDITIONING Stand in deep water for several hours.

Pyrus **Pear**
Trees with white blossom in spring, and yellow or green fruit in autumn.
MEANING Affection.
AVAILABILITY Blossom: spring. Fruit: autumn. All year from greengrocers.
PLANTING CONDITIONS Any soil. Sun.
CONDITIONING Hammer woody stems, then stand in deep water for several hours. Home-grown fruit lasts longer.

Ranunculus **Buttercup**
Apart from the native yellow varieties, there are many other larger, brightly coloured forms with double flowers.

AVAILABILITY Summer. Florists: most of the year.
PLANTING CONDITIONS Very well-drained soil. Full sun.
CONDITIONING Stand in deep water for several hours.

Raphanus **Radish**
Useful for the red and white roots which can be globular or tubular.
AVAILABILITY Spring, summer and autumn. All year from greengrocers.
PLANTING CONDITIONS Any soil. Sun or light shade.

Rheum **Rhubarb**
The young leaves can be used from the culinary and ornamental rhubarbs before they get too old.
MEANING Advice.
AVAILABILITY Spring.
PLANTING CONDITIONS Moist, rich soil. Full sun or light shade.
CONDITIONING Submerge whole leaf for several hours.

Rhododendron
A very large family of evergreen shrubs with clusters of yellow, white, pink, red and purple flowers.
MEANING Danger.
AVAILABILITY Winter to autumn.
PLANTING CONDITIONS Lime-free soil. Partial shade.
CONDITIONING Hammer woody stems, then stand in deep water for several hours.

Ribes **Flowering currant**
Deciduous shrubs with hanging clusters of small, pink or red flowers and fresh, heavily veined leaves. Can be forced.
MEANING Thy frown will kill me.
AVAILABILITY Spring.
PLANTING CONDITIONS Any soil. Sun or light shade.
CONDITIONING Hammer woody stems, then stand in deep water for several hours.

Rosa **Rose**
A very large family of shrubs and climbers with a good range of colours. Many are fragrant and the majority have thorny stems.
MEANING Love.
AVAILABILITY Summer and autumn. Florists: all year.
PLANTING CONDITIONS Any soil. Sun.
CONDITIONING Best cut in bud. Stand in deep water for several hours.

Rosmarinus **Rosemary**
Evergreen shrubs with small needle-like, grey leaves which are fragrant when crushed. Pale blue flowers.
MEANING Remembrance.
AVAILABILITY Foliage: all year. Flowers: summer and autumn.
PLANTING CONDITIONS Any soil. Sun.
CONDITIONING Crush woody stems, then stand in deep water for several hours.

Rubus **Blackberry, bramble**
Thorny rambling shrubs with mauve

flowers and black berries, both often being borne at the same time.
MEANING Lowliness, envy, remorse.
AVAILABILITY Autumn.
PLANTING CONDITIONS Any soil. Sun or light shade.
CONDITIONING Hammer woody stems then stand in deep water for several hours.

Rudbeckia **Coneflower, black-eyed Susan**
Bright yellow, orange and brown daisy-like flowers with long rough stems. Single or double. Last well in water.
AVAILABILITY Late summer and autumn.
PLANTING CONDITIONS Any soil. Sun.
CONDITIONING Boil stems and stand in deep water for several hours.

Ruscus **Butcher's broom, box holly**
Curious shrubs with modified stems that look like sharp-pointed leaves, the centre of which carry bright red berries after insignificant flowers.
AVAILABILITY Foliage: all year. Berries: autumn.
PLANTING CONDITIONS Any soil. Shade.
CONDITIONING Hammer woody stems, then stand in deep water for several hours.

Ruta **Rue**
Shrubby herbs with deeply cut, blue-grey leaves which are very aromatic. The flowers are yellow but not used much in arrangements.
MEANING Grief, disdain.
AVAILABILITY Summer and autumn.
PLANTING CONDITIONS Any soil. Sun.
CONDITIONING Crush woody stems, then stand in deep water for several hours.

Saintpaulia **African violet**
Very popular house plants with dark green, furry leaves and blue or purple flowers on short stems. Last quite well in water or use as pot plants.
AVAILABILITY All year.
PLANTING CONDITIONS Greenhouse or conservatory.
CONDITIONING Stand in deep water for several hours.

Salix **Willow, pussy willow**
Trees and shrubs with variation in bark colour, useful during winter. Most also bear interesting catkins.
MEANING Freedom, mourning.
AVAILABILITY Stems: winter. Catkins: late winter and spring. Foliage: spring to autumn.
PLANTING CONDITIONS Sun. Moisture-retentive soils.
CONDITIONING Hammer woody stems, then stand in deep water for several hours.

Salvia **Sage**
Shrubs and herbaceous perennials with long spikes of blue or purple flowers. Foliage often aromatic. Last quite well in water.
MEANING Domestic virtue, esteem.
AVAILABILITY Summer and autumn.

PLANTING CONDITIONS Any soil. Sun.
CONDITIONING Stand in deep water for several hours.

Sambucus **Elder**
Deciduous shrubs with large flat-headed clusters of white flowers. Many have interesting foliage, which can be purple, golden or variegated. Some have very finely cut leaves.
MEANING Zealousness.
AVAILABILITY Flowers: spring. Foliage: spring to autumn. Berries: autumn.
PLANTING CONDITIONS Any soil. Sun or light shade.
CONDITIONING Hammer woody stems, then stand in deep water for several hours.

Santolina **Lavender cotton**
Small evergreen shrubs with aromatic green or grey stems and foliage. Summer flowers are yellow but of little consequence.
AVAILABILITY All year.
PLANTING CONDITIONS Any soil. Full sun.
CONDITIONING Hammer woody stems, then stand in deep water for several hours.

Scabiosa **Scabious, pincushion flower**
Blue, mauve, white or pale yellow disc-shaped flowers. There are double varieties available. Last quite well in water.
MEANING Unfortunate love.
AVAILABILITY Summer.
PLANTING CONDITIONS Any soil. Sun.
CONDITIONING Stand in deep water for several hours.

Scilla **Squill**
Short-stemmed bulbs with star-like flowers in blue, violet or white.
AVAILABILITY Spring.
PLANTING CONDITIONS Any soil. Sun.
CONDITIONING Stand in deep water for several hours.

Sedum **Stonecrop**
Fleshy succulent plants with flat heads of red, pink or mauve. Also smaller varieties with white or yellow flowers.
MEANING Tranquillity.
AVAILABILITY Autumn.
PLANTING CONDITIONS Any soil. Full sun.
CONDITIONING Stand in deep water for several hours.

Senecio **Ragwort, cineraria**
Yellow daisy-like flowers with valuable green or grey foliage. Cineraria are brightly coloured and used as pot plants.
AVAILABILITY Summer.
PLANTING CONDITIONS Any soil. Sun.
CONDITIONING Crush woody stems, then stand in deep water for several hours.

Skimmia
Evergreen shrubs with glossy leaves and clusters of long lasting red berries. White scented flowers. Last well in water.
AVAILABILITY Foliage: all year. Flowers:

spring. Berries: autumn to spring.
PLANTING CONDITIONS Lime-free soil. Sun or light shade. Both male and female required to get berries.
CONDITIONING Hammer woody stems, then stand in deep water for several hours.

Solanum Winter cherry
Small trees or bushes grown in pots for their bright orange or red berries.
AVAILABILITY Winter.
PLANTING CONDITIONS Warm greenhouse or conservatory.

Solidago Golden rod
Long-stemmed plants with fluffy, feathery yellow plumes. Last quite well in water.
MEANING Precaution.
AVAILABILITY Summer and autumn.
PLANTING CONDITIONS Any soil. Sun.
CONDITIONING Stand in deep water for several hours.

Sorbus Mountain ash, rowan
Deciduous trees which are useful for the clusters of white flowers, silvery foliage which has good autumn tints and orange, pink or white berries.
MEANING Prudence.
AVAILABILITY Flowers: spring. Foliage: summer or autumn. Berries: autumn.
PLANTING CONDITIONS Any soil. Sun or light shade.
CONDITIONING Hammer woody stems, then stand in deep water for several hours.

Spiraea
Deciduous shrubs with masses of small white or pink flowers either in sprays or flat heads. There are variegated-leaved forms.
AVAILABILITY Spring.
PLANTING CONDITIONS Any soil. Sun or light shade.
CONDITIONING Hammer woody stems, then stand in deep water for several hours.

Stachys Lamb's ears
Herbaceous plants with soft, felty, grey or silver leaves and pale pink flowers on tallish grey stems.
AVAILABILITY Summer and autumn.
PLANTING CONDITIONS Any soil. Sunny position.
CONDITIONING Stand in water for several hours, being careful not to overwet the foliage.

Staphylea Bladdernut
Deciduous shrubs with clusters of white, scented flowers in summer followed by curious, translucent seed capsules which seem to be inflated.
MEANING Frivolity, amusement.
AVAILABILITY Flowers: summer. Seed capsules: autumn.
PLANTING CONDITIONS Most soils. Sun.
CONDITIONING Hammer woody stems, then stand in deep water for several hours.

Stranvaesia
Semi-deciduous shrubs with red

leaves about to fall contrasting well with the green ones staying on the plant. Contrast also helped by clusters of red berries.
AVAILABILITY Autumn.
PLANTING CONDITIONS Any soil. Sun or light shade.
CONDITIONING Hammer woody stems, then stand in deep water for several hours.

Strelitzia Bird of paradise flower
Tender brightly coloured plants whose flower resembles the head of a bird with a bright orange crest.
AVAILABILITY Spring. All year from florists.
PLANTING CONDITIONS Warm greenhouse or conservatory.
CONDITIONING Stand in deep water for several hours.

Symphoricarpos Snowberry
Deciduous shrubs with insignificant pink flowers that produce white berries, which stay on the naked stems.
AVAILABILITY Autumn and winter.
PLANTING CONDITIONS Any soil. Sun or shade.
CONDITIONING Hammer woody stems, then stand in deep water for several hours.

Syringa Lilac
Deciduous shrubs with large spikes of fragrant flowers in white and varying shades of mauve and purple.
MEANING White: first emotions of love. Mauve: youthful innocence.
AVAILABILITY Spring.
PLANTING CONDITIONS Any soil. Sun or light shade.
CONDITIONING Hammer woody stems, then stand in deep water for several hours.

Taxus Yew
Evergreen conifers with dark green, narrow leaves. Also attractive, sticky red fruit in autumn. Some think it unlucky if brought into the house. Last very well in water.
MEANING Sorrow.
AVAILABILITY Foliage: all year.
PLANTING CONDITIONS Any soil. Sun or shade.
CONDITIONING Hammer woody stems, then stand in deep water for several hours.

Thalictrum Meadow rue
Tall plants with sprays of fluffy, yellow, mauve or purple flowers. The delicate foliage is finely cut and can be green, grey-green or blue-green.
AVAILABILITY Summer.
PLANTING CONDITIONS Any soil. Sun or light shade.
CONDITIONING Stand in deep water for several hours.

Thymus Thyme
Dwarf shrubby herbs which are very fragrant, particularly if crushed. Pink, mauve or purple flowers on short stems.

MEANING Activity.
AVAILABILITY Summer.
PLANTING CONDITIONS Well-drained soil. Full sun.
CONDITIONING Stand in deep water for several hours.

Tricyrtis Toad lily
Sprays of intriguing white, mauve or yellow flowers, with heavy purple spotting, on tall arching stems. Last well in water.
AVAILABILITY Autumn.
PLANTING CONDITIONS Moist, woodland conditions. Shade.
CONDITIONING Stand in deep water for several hours.

Trollius Globe flower
Yellow or orange flower reminiscent of a large, double buttercup.
AVAILABILITY Late spring, early summer.
PLANTING CONDITIONS Light shade. Moisture-retentive soil.
CONDITIONING Dip stem ends in boiling water, then stand in deep water for several hours.

Tropaeolum Nasturtium
Annual climbing plants with vivid orange or red trumpets. Also more tender varieties needing winter protection. Last well in water.
MEANING Patriotism.
AVAILABILITY Summer, autumn.
PLANTING CONDITIONS Any soil. Sun. Need support.
CONDITIONING Stand in deep water for several hours.

Tulipa Tulip
Familiar bulbous plants with brightly coloured chalices in a wide range of colours including near-black. Long lasting in water.
MEANING Fame.
AVAILABILITY Spring and summer. Also winter from florists.
PLANTING CONDITIONS Any soil. Sunny position.
CONDITIONING Stand in deep water for several hours.

Verbena
A large range of annual and perennial plants mainly pink, mauve and purple. Some are short-stemmed but others are very tall (V. bonariensis). Some are scented. Last very well in water.
AVAILABILITY Summer and autumn.
PLANTING CONDITIONS Any soil. Sunny position.
CONDITIONING Stand in deep water for several hours.

Viburnum
Evergreen and deciduous shrubs with white or pink flowers, often heavily scented.
AVAILABILITY Winter, spring and autumn.
PLANTING CONDITIONS Most soils. Sunny position.
CONDITIONING Hammer woody stems, then stand in deep water for several hours.

Vinca Periwinkle
Evergreen trailing shrubs with blue, mauve or white flowers. V. difformis has white or pale-blue flowers in mid-winter.
MEANING Blue: early friendship. White: pleasures of memory.
AVAILABILITY Winter, spring and summer.
PLANTING CONDITIONS Any soil. Shady position.
CONDITIONING Stand in deep water for several hours.

Viola Pansy, viola, violet
Varying sizes of the well-known viola-shaped flowers in a wide range of colours. All are short-stemmed. Some are fragrant.
MEANING Pansy: thoughts. Violet: faithfulness, watchfulness, modesty.
AVAILABILITY Spring to autumn. Some pansies all year.
PLANTING CONDITIONS Any soil. Light shade or sun.
CONDITIONING Stand in deep water for several hours.

Vitis Grape, vine
Can be used for the foliage, particularly with autumn colour, or for the fruit.
MEANING Charity.
AVAILABILITY Autumn.
PLANTING CONDITIONS Any soil. Sun or light shade. Fruit all year from greengrocers.
CONDITIONING Foliage: Boil stem ends, then stand in deep water for several hours. Fruit: avoid removing the bloom.

Zantedeschia Arum lily, calla lily
Pure white, folded trumpets with a central spike. Large glossy leaves. Some people regard them as being funereal. Pink and yellow varieties also available.
AVAILABILITY Spring and early summer.
PLANTING CONDITIONS Sun. Moisture-retentive soil. Some varieties need winter protection.
CONDITIONING Stand in deep water for several hours.

Zea Corn-on-the-cob, Indian corn, maize, sweet corn
Grass with large leaves and large yellow seed-heads wrapped in green and topped with soft tassels.
AVAILABILITY Autumn.
PLANTING CONDITIONS Any soil. Sunny position.

Zinnia
Very colourful annuals with large double, daisy-like flower-heads. Yellow, orange, red, purple and white available. Last well in water.
MEANING Thoughts of absent friends.
AVAILABILITY Summer and autumn.
PLANTING CONDITIONS Any soil. Sunny position.
CONDITIONING Stand in deep water for several hours.

NATIONAL TRUST PLACES OF INTEREST

Houses noted for their flower arrangements

Blickling Hall Norfolk
Large vases of cut flowers from the garden arranged by the garden staff.

Castle Ward County Down
Bold arrangements made by the guides and administrator's wife.

Chartwell Kent
Lady Churchill's favourite white- and pale-coloured flowers are still grown in the garden, and simple arrangements placed around the house as they were in her time. Similarly, plants and bulbs are raised in the greenhouses, including large bowls of the brightly coloured amaryllis lilies admired by Sir Winston.

Dyrham Park Avon
Simple, large-scale cut flowers and foliage arranged by the administrator's wife and provided by the gardener from the cutting border. The orangery of 1700 is just about frost-free and provides pot plants, including camelias at Easter, clivia and lilies later on.

Haddo House Aberdeenshire
All through the season, 25 vases of fresh flowers are arranged by Lady Aberdeen, using flowers grown in the garden; also three very large dried-flower arrangements situated in the entrance hall and staircase.

Kedleston Hall Derbyshire
Good flower arrangements in most of the rooms, arranged by the volunteer stewards, following the tradition of the Curzon family.

Killerton Devon
Good flower arrangements throughout the house, including

flowers in a reproduction eighteenth-century, pyramid cut-flower container.

Petworth House Sussex
Large bowls of mixed cut flowers arranged by the administrator's wife in the style and taste set by Pamela, Lady Egremont in the 1960s. Posies of fresh flowers are always on the dressing tables in the bedrooms.

Waddesdon Manor Buckinghamshire
Flowers continue to be a great feature of the house. They are sent from Mrs de Rothschild's garden and arranged by one of her gardeners. There are large arrangements in most rooms.

Wightwick Manor Wolverhampton
All the flower arrangements made by Mr Frederick Clegg FRHS, one of the guides, who writes and lectures for the RHS. He grows all the flowers in his own small garden; many are unusual and old varieties, which appear in pre-Raphaelite paintings and William Morris designs. Ardress House, County Armagh, Benthall Hall and Dudmaston in Shropshire, Knightshayes Court, Devon, and Westwood Manor, Wiltshire, always have good flower arrangements.

Houses that display floral decorations at Christmas

Blickling Hall Norfolk
Cotehele, Lanhydrock Cornwall
Shugborough Staffordshire
Tatton Park Cheshire
Wightwick Manor Wolverhampton

Gardens with borders planted specifically for cutting

Ascott Buckinghamshire
Calke Abbey Derbyshire (not open until 1989)
Chartwell Kent (also greenhouses)
Chirk Castle Clwyd
Cotehele Cornwall
Dyrham Park Avon
Felbrigg Hall Norfolk (in the walled garden)
Fenton House London
Grey's Court Oxfordshire
Gunby Hall Lincolnshire
Hardwick Hall Derbyshire
Lindisfarne Castle Northumberland (walled garden designed by Gertrude Jekyll)
Nymans West Sussex (greenhouses)
Oxburgh Hall Norfolk
Packwood House Warwickshire
Peckover House Cambridgeshire
Petworth West Sussex
Saltram Devon
Scotney Castle Kent (the castle is now ruined)
Sizergh Castle Cumbria
Tatton Park Cheshire
Tintinhull Wiltshire
Wallington Northumberland (in the walled garden)

Rose gardens

Ardress County Armagh
Ascott Buckinghamshire
Barrington Court Somerset (designed by Gertrude Jekyll)
Basildon Park Berkshire
Bateman's E Sussex (planned and planted by Rudyard Kipling)
Blickling Hall Norfolk
Bodnant Gwynedd (terrace)
Castle Drogo Devon

Chartwell Kent (planted by Lady Churchill)
Chirk Castle Clwyd
Cliveden Buckinghamshire (designed by Geoffrey Jellicoe for Lord and Lady Astor)
Cotehele Cornwall
Emmetts Kent
Farnborough Hall Warwickshire
Fenton House London
Florence Court County Fermanagh
Grey's Court Oxfordshire
Gunby Hall Lincolnshire
Hardwick Hall Derbyshire
Hidcote Manor Gloucestershire
Hughenden Manor Buckinghamshire (once home of Benjamin Disraeli)
Lamb House East Sussex (once home of Henry James)
Lanhydrock Cornwall
Lyme Park Cheshire
Lytes Cary Manor Somerset
Mottisfont Abbey Hampshire (national collection of ancestral species and nineteenth century cultivars)
Nymans West Sussex (old shrub roses)
Peckover Cambridgeshire
Polesden Lacey Surrey (Edwardian rose garden laid out by Mrs Greville)
Powis Castle Powys
Rufford Old Hall Lancashire
Shugborough Staffordshire (Victorian-style rose garden created by the Trust in 1966)
Sissinghurst Kent
Tatton Park Cheshire
Upton House Warwickshire
Waddesdon Manor Buckinghamshire
Wightwick Manor West Midlands

ACKNOWLEDGMENTS

The author would like to thank: Sarah Franklyn, Charlotte Fraser, Jenny Raworth and Celia Rugg for all their wonderful help with plant material; Amalgam, London SW13; Kate Dyson at The Dining Room Shop, London SW13; Studio 92, London SW13; special thanks are due to Sue Newth and all the cast at Hillier and Hilton; and to Val Austin, May Cristea, Kathleen Darby, Peter Day, Lena Harries, Veronica Hitchcock, Alex Starkie and Roddy Wood for their valuable support.

Dorling Kindersley would like to thank: Hilary and Richard Bird for the index; Kate Grant for invaluable help with the typing; Carol Kenwright and staff at Ightham Mote; Anthony Lord at the National Trust and Richard Bird for authenticating plant names; Claudine Meissner for design work; Sue Mennell for picture research; Canon John Morris and staff at Saint Mary's Church, Battersea, London; Charles Settrington and staff at Settrington Studios; Christian Tumpling for photographic work; and Mr and Mrs A Norton, Denis L Flower CBE, Mrs A L Hutchinson and Miss S L Leaning, Mr and Mrs M Furniss, Mrs Sybil B Spencer and Liz Cooke for photography in their gardens.

Photographic credits
All photography by Stephen Hayward except for: Linda Burgess p. 227; Dorling Kindersley Garden Library pp. 115, 131, 155, 173; Jacqui Hurst pp. 224, 228, 231, 232, 235, 236, 239.

Black-and-white line illustrations
Mary Evans Picture Library pp. 10, 24, 33, 67, 78, 91, 96, 117, 118, 119, 128, 198, 241; Anne Ronan Picture Library pp. 55, 61, 75; Royal Horticultural Society/Lindley Library pp. 6, 12, 26, 58, 74, 86, 106, 133–141, 156–161, 174, 175; Amoret Tanner pp. 33, 57, 70, 71, 73, 96, 190, 241–252.

Illustrators
David Ashby pp. 38–41, 44, 45, 48; Jane Cradock-Watson pp. 34–37; Sheilagh Noble – all illuminated letters; Sandra Pond and Will Giles pp. 42, 43, 46, 47.

Ceramics
Sandy Brown p. 145; Derek Davis p. 238; Julian King-Salter p. 76; Colin Pearson pp. 180–181; Janice Tchalenko p. 153; Robin Welch p. 23.